6/22

THIS PUBLICATION MADE POSSIBLE BY

Mr. & Mrs. Thomas B. Preston

Jack & Peggy Browder
Major General Frederick A. Daugherty (Ret.)
Senator Charles R. Ford
Mrs. Rene (Eva) Gerard
Richard & Helen Horton
Norman Jonas
Governor & Mrs. Frank Keating
Leonard M. Logan iv
John Massey
C. R. Musgrave, Jr.
Margaret Riney Trust
Lew & Myra Ward

Mr. & Mrs. Walter Allison
Warren R. Anderson
Sharon Garrison Ausloos
Molly & David Boren
Mr. & Mrs. Donald H. Creel
Charles & Julie Daniels
Willene B. Douce
Mrs. M. W. "Bud" Eddleman
LeRoy H. & Martha G. Fischer
Mr. & Mrs. Martin Garber, Jr.
Jessie Garrison
Michael Eric Goldstein
Heather & Dick Grisham
Bill Gustafson
Mr. & Mrs. Henry Kane
Richard Kane
Faye & Charles Kittrell
Carolyn & Forrest Lowrance
Dr. & Mrs. V. M. Lockard
Lloyd Lynd
William B. & Anita S. Mackenzie
Larry G. Markel
Joe & Carol McGraw
Commander Roger G. Pyle
Emmy Scott Stidham
Dr. & Mrs. Lewis Stiles
Mrs. Wiiliam R. Sumter
Mr. & Mrs. John S. Van Aken
Mr. & Mrs. W. Robert Wilson

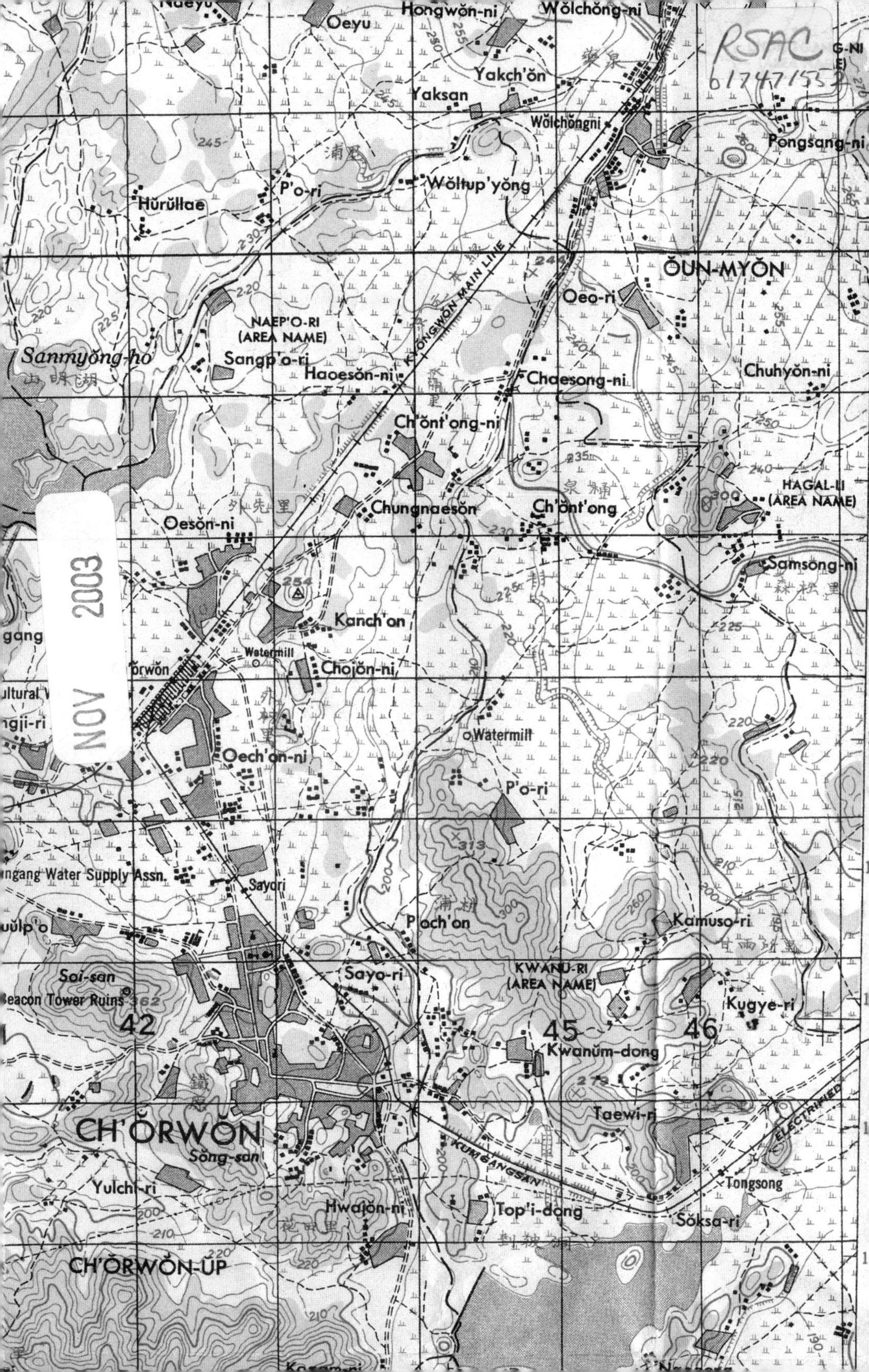
RSAC
61747155?
NOV 2003
Hongwŏn-ni
Wŏlchŏng-ni
Oeyu
Yakch'ŏn
Yaksan
Wŏlchŏngni
Pongsang-ni
P'o-ri
Wŏltup'yŏng
Hŭrŭllae
ŎUN-MYŎN
Oeo-ri
NAEP'O-RI
(AREA NAME)
Sanmyŏng-ho
Sangp'o-ri
Haoesŏn-ni
Chaesong-ni
Chuhyŏn-ni
KYŎNGWŎN MAIN LINE
Ch'ŏnt'ong-ni
HAGAL-LI
(AREA NAME)
Chungnaesŏn
Ch'ŏnt'ong
Oesŏn-ni
Samsong-ni
Kanch'on
Watermill
Chojŏn-ni
Watermill
Oech'on-ni
P'o-ri
Water Supply Assn.
Sayori
P'och'on
Kamuso-ri
Soi-san
Beacon Tower Ruins
Sayo-ri
KWANU-RI
(AREA NAME)
Kugye-ri
42
45
46
Kwanŭm-dong
Taewi-ri
CH'ŎRWŎN
Sŏng-san
KUMGANGSAN
ELECTRIFIED
Yulchi-ri
Tongsong
Hwajŏn-ni
Top'i-dong
Sŏksa-ri
CH'ŎRWŎN-ŬP

REMEMBRANCES OF A REDLEG

DENZIL D. GARRISON

The story of A KOREAN WAR ARTILLERYMAN

of the 45TH THUNDERBIRD DIVISION

SERIES EDITOR: KENNY A. FRANKS

ASSOCIATE EDITOR: GINI MOORE CAMPBELL

OKLAHOMA HERITAGE ASSOCIATION / OKLAHOMA CITY

LC Number 2002116905
ISBN 1-885596-31-6
Design by Carol Haralson

Printed in Canada

OKLAHOMA HERITAGE ASSOCIATION
201 N.W. 14th Street
Oklahoma City, Oklahoma 73103

Jacket cover: A 105mm howitzer of Battery "B," 171st Field artillery battalion, of the 45th Thunderbird Division firing on the enemy during the Korean War.

Back cover: First Lieutenant Denzil D. Garrison. In the jacket photo Garrison's hand rests on a book about his ancestor, Isaac Garrison (1732-1836), a soldier in the Revolutionary War.

DEDICATED TO ALL THE THUNDERBIRDS,
PAST, PRESENT, AND FUTURE,
ESPECIALLY THE FOLLOWING,
WHO ARE NO LONGER WITH US.

Dallas L. Boren
Jack M. Buckley
Edgar J. "Boodle" Conn
James M. Crabtree
Harold D. Davis
John T. Dunn
Morgan W. Eddleman
Joseph Don Garrison, Sr.
Joseph Don Garrison, Jr.
William C. Garrison
Harry W. Hughes
Alvin L. Latimer
Ernest T. McKean
Fred T. Mitchell
Hal L. Muldrow, Jr.
William E. "Perc" Murphy
James A. Nolan
Paul W. Reed, Jr.
Ellis B. Richie
Joseph F. Rolette
James O. Smith
James C. Styron
William R. Sumter
LaVern Weber
Donald P. Younce
and all the rest.

The ranks of World War II and Korean Thunderbirds are thinning quickly. Please remember them.

CONTENTS

FOREWORD

Denzil Garrison's inspiring history of artillerymen of the 45th Thunderbird Division during the Korea War could not be more timely. Since the terrorist attacks upon our country on September 11, 2002, many of us have thought a great deal about what it means to be an American. This book helps to answer that question.

Shortly after September 11, I was asked a question by a student in class which I teach at Denzil Garrison's alma mater, the University of Oklahoma. The question was "Will there always be any America?" The student had never in her lifetime seen her home country under attack. She was frightened. She worried that we might ultimately collapse like other powerful nations in the past. As I answered her question by expressing my own faith in the future of our country, I began to think about what it means to be an American. Many nations and peoples are defined in almost tribal terms. Generally they define themselves in terms of being of the same race, or of the same religion, or in terms of speaking the same native language from birth. They gain their identity from sharing the same cultural history. America is unique. We come from many places. Americans are of different cultural backgrounds and come from homes where many languages are spoken. We are of many races and are diverse in our religious perspectives. We are defined instead by our common belief in freedom and in the rights and dignity of all human beings. It is our shared ideals and values that make us Americans. The answer to the student's question is that there will always be an America as long as we care enough to protect and defend those values and as long as we live by them.

Remembrances of a Redleg is a story of a group of Americans from the famed Thunderbird Division who answered the call to protect and defend our freedom. From the cities and the small towns and farms mainly from Oklahoma, rich and poor, businessmen, farmers, mechanics, teachers, students and others from all walks of life, they set aside their own work and plans to answer the call to duty. While many of those in the 171st Field Artillery Battalion were Oklahomans, they quickly welcomed those from other parts of the country who joined their ranks. The unit represented many different racial groups. Garrison writes eloquently of the leadership displayed by native American soldiers. He recounts the way in which African Americans were accepted into the unit as replacement troops. It was the first time that many of the soldiers had ever fought and lived side by side with black Americans. The unit's Native American first sergeant quietly told his men that every new replacement would be treated with "The respect that he was due as an American soldier." There was full compliance with the sergeant's directives and the integration of the unit became a point of pride for those who shared the experience. As Garrison explained, they were all Americans too busy working together to fight a war to worry about Jim Crowism.

The book is filled with acts of great courage like those of Harry Hughes, a hero of both World War II and the Korean War and Gene Short who made his way across a minefield to save Garrisons life. It takes us to locations like "Old Baldy" and "Pork Chop Hill" which will be long remembered in American military history.

As an Oklahoman I am especially grateful that this book has been written. The 45th Division, known as the Thunderbirds was comprised mainly of Oklahomans. It was in combat for 511 days in Europe during World War II and was in combat for 429 days in the Korean War. General George Patton called the 45th one of the best divisions in the history of American Arms.

Anyone who has ever worn the Thunderbird patch has worn it as a badge of honor. I have always felt especially privileged to be an

Oklahoman. Because we are a young state many of us alive today have been privileged to know the great figures of our history. They have passed on to us the special spirit of our state where every person has a chance to prove himself or herself. Oklahoma is a place where what you are and what you stand for is much more important than who your ancestors might have been. That spirit and the concern which we have for each other as members of one American family are expressed on every page of this book.

Many of the names listed in this book are far more than just names to me. These men were friends and mentors who had a major impact on my life like Colonel J.O. "Cotton" Smith and his son Jerry who helped me get started in public life, General LaVern Weber who guided me to join the Oklahoma National Guard which gave me the privilege of wearing the Thunderbird patch, General Hal Muldrow, Paul Reed and a host of others. It will always be a matter of pride to me and to my family that my much-loved uncle, Dallas Boren, served as unit chaplain.

The author of the book, Denzil D. Garrison, modestly assumes the role of narrator, always understanding his own part in the action. He too is a true representative of the best of the American spirit. I first met Denny Garrison in 1967 when he was a State Senator. He had already been county attorney of Washington Country and a member of the legislature for several years having served as Minority Leader of both the Oklahoma State House of Representatives and the Oklahoma State Senate. While we were in different political parties he extended his friendship to me from my very first day as a freshman state representative. I quickly learned that he had the courage of his convictions and that he was very willing to work across party lines to serve the public interests. We both ran for Governor in 1974. That contest only enhanced my respect for his personal integrity and ability. After I became Governor of Oklahoma in 1975 I asked him to help me as staff coordinator of legislative programs so that we could work together to help our state on a bipartisan basis. Just as he answered the call to duty setting aside his law school studies to go to Korea, he put aside his own political ambitions to serve on my staff. As a young governor with far less political experience than Denny Garrison, I greatly benefited from his help and wise counsel. Now as President of the University of Oklahoma, I live in Norman where he grew up and am privileged to work at the university from which he graduated and where he met his very special wife Barbara.

It has been said that the strength of our democracy for more than two centuries is remarkable because in a sense, a democracy like ours has to be built and rebuilt by every succeeding generation. Each generation in its turn must believe in the value of freedom and individual human rights. Each must be prepared to participate in our society and to give of time and talent to make it better and pass on enhanced opportunities to the next generation. Each generation must be prepared to sacrifice personal security and even life itself to protect and preserve it.

This book is a fitting tribute to those brave Thunderbirds who served in the Korean War. It is also a great gift to the generations which will follow them. It will help them better understand what it means to be an American. It will help them understand that as long as there are those who cherish freedom and understand its full meaning, there will always be an America. No military power and no act of terrorism can destroy the values which define us and bind us together.

DAVID L. BOREN, PRESIDENT
UNIVERSITY OF OKLAHOMA

ACKNOWLEDGMENTS

The author extends special thanks to the following persons and entities that contributed priceless photographs, support, and memories in the creation of this book: David N. Beckwermert, David L. Boren, Mrs. Morgan W. Eddleman, the children of Joseph Don Garrison, Jr., Frank T. Fleet, James R. Jack, Jerry T. McElroy, Ernest T. McKean, Nicholas B. O'Reilly, Mrs. Paul W. Reed, Jr., Blair E. Rollin, Edward Saunders, Raymond J. Scoufos, Donald J. Stacey, James T. Steidley, Harold Winburn, 45th Infantry Division Museum, Laurie Garrison Photography, the Oklahoma Historical Society, and the Oklahoma Heritage Association.

In addition, the author would like to thank editors Kenny A. Franks and Gini Moore Campbell of the Oklahoma Heritage Association for their continued efforts in preserving Oklahoma's incredible history. Thanks to designer Carol Haralson for using her talents in bringing this book to life.

Finally, a special thanks to Blake Wade and Dr. Bob Blackburn, without whose help this book would never have been written and published.

Redleg is an old army name for an artilleryman. The name came from the red stripe on the outer seam of artillery soldiers' uniform trousers. That stripe distinguished the artillerymen from soldiers of other branches. The name has been used to describe artillery soldiers since the Civil War. In later years, horse artillerymen wore laced leather boots, which had a decided red tinge. This probably caused the term to become a permanent part of soldiers' vocabulary.

CHAPTER 1

THE RETREADS RETURN

The weather was stifling, and the work was hard. We were repainting an old grade school that had been built in 1902, in my hometown of Norman, Oklahoma. Up on a scaffold, the heavy sprayer seemed to weigh a thousand pounds. My shoulders ached, and I longed to be through with that disagreeable job. To keep us company, the old custodian and I listened to a portable radio, which we used to make the hours pass faster as we sprayed paint. Mostly, we just listened to music all day. However, on 25 June 1950, the regular program was interrupted by a news bulletin announcing that the People's Democratic Republic of Korea, commonly called North Korea had just invaded the Republic of Korea or South Korea. I listened intently, and after the bulletin, I hung up my sprayer for good. I announced to my co-worker that I was leaving. He asked, "Where are you going?" I answered, "To Korea." As things worked out, I was right.

Entering the Army in the latter part of World War II, I attended basic training in the field artillery, at Fort Sill, Oklahoma, and immediately after that, entered Field Artillery Officer's Candidate School (OCS) there at "Sill," as we called it. Upon graduation and commissioning as a second lieutenant of field artillery, I went to Germany, where the war was just ending. After a year spent in the Army of Occupation, I returned to my home in Norman, where I started to prepare for law school. Admitted into Oklahoma University Law School in 1948, I was just about to start my senior year of law studies

Members of Battery B, 171st Field Artillery Battalion, August 6, 1951. *Left to right, first row:* 2nd Lieutenant George Chesnut, Warrant Officer Junior Grade Ernest T. McKean, 1st Sergeant John T. Dunn, First Lieutenant Denzil D. Garrison, 2nd Lieutenant Edgar J. Bradshaw, 2nd Lieutenant William R. Sumter, 1st Lieutenant James M. Crabtree. *Second row:* Private 1st Class Wayne R. Wolfe, Corporal Norman D. Patterson, Sergeant 1st Class Harold D. Davis, Sergeant 1st Class Fred T. Mitchell, Sergeant 1st Class Charles J. Brown, Master Sergeant Herbert L. Tash, Sergeant 1st Class Jimmie E. Dunn, Sergeant 1st Class Samuel T. Bullard, Sergeant 1st Class Claron H. Coleman, Sergeant 1st Class Edgar M. Cox, Sergeant 1st Class Floyd K. Clark, Sergeant 1st Class John L. Cloyd, Private 1st Class Benjamin F. Hicks, Private 1st Class Euen G. Savage, Private 1st Class George K. White. *Third row:* Private Ralph Persechino, Private Ralph A. Patrone, Private 1st Class John V. Allen, Private Angelo Barone, Sergeant Donald J. Stacey, Sergeant Dennis A. Smith Jr., Sergeant Dale W. Cannon, Private "Frog" Cunningham, Sergeant Wilfred Pate, Sergeant William R. Epps, Sergeant Walter V. Allison, Corporal Gus Doyle, Sergeant James L. Steidley, Sergeant Jack L. Shannon, Private 1st Class John J. Pitts, Private 1st Class Harold G. Wills, Private 1st Class Peter M. Iozzio. *Fourth row:* Private 1st Class Arvel H. Woessner, Corporal John W. Van de Kamp, Sergeant Louis S. Cioni, Private 1st Class Sam C. Oda, Private 1st Class Dan Biondi, Corporal Willie E. Burns, Corporal Lawrence A. Mack, Private 1st Class Earl D. Bloom, Corporal Harold D. Gustin, Corporal Herbert H. Bunch, Corporal Marshall E. Wilson, Private 1st Class Leonardo de Mola, Private Morton Nosenchuk, Private 1st Class John P. Gregory, Private Milton K. Daily, Private 1st Class Norman C. Lloyd, Private 1st Class Paul M. Gorsky, Private Paul L. Vargo, Private 1st Class Winfred M. Smith, Corporal Robert L. Wittenberger. *Fifth row:* Corporal Max O. Grantham, Private 1st Class

Donald Lunt, Corporal Leon E. Parker, Corporal Norbert Bochsler, Corporal Richard V. Bruneau, Private 1st Class, Edward J. Donelan, Private 1st Class Charles L. Smith, Private Nicholas B. O'Reilly, Corporal Bill D. Geter, Private Edward J. O'Donnell, Private 1st Class Glenn Rundquist, Corporal James J. Murphy, Private 1st Class Donovan E. Blough, Private 1st Class Thomas C. Gruell, Private 1st Class Walter A. Goll, Private 1st Class Alfred B. Edwards, Private 1st Class John G. Bradley, Private 1st Class Glenn Harvill, Private 1st Class James McCracken. *Sixth row:* Corporal Francis C. Hansen, Private 1st Class William H. Hastings, Corporal Loyd S. DeWeese, Corporal William T. Henderson, Private 1st Class Murray Gruper, Private Walter J. Newman, Private 1st Class Wilbur L. Brown, Private Louis Nardo, Private 1st Class Alton O. Vatne, Private 1st Class Richard S. McLaughlin, Corporal Doyle C. Payne, Corporal George W. Lematta, Private 1st Class Norman G. Wright, Private 1st Class Orlind S. Case, Private 1st Class Agostine S. Petrillo, Private Sheldon Pachtman, Private 1st Class Kenneth N. Hads, Private 1st Class Ralph A Walter. *Back row:* Private 1st Class Donald P. Younce, Private 1st Class Antonio Chiodi, Private 1st Class Anthony T. Gallo, Private 1st Class Hilmen Svaleson, Private 1st Class Andrew Zabrodsky, Corporal George J. O'Brien, Corporal John Brix, Sergeant Hugh E. Barnett, Private 1st Class William E. Horster, Private 1st Class Jerry T. McElroy, Sergeant Jesse C. McGee, Private 1st Class Dean R. Mink, Private Orgie C. Farmer, Corporal James McLeod, Private 1st Class Donald P. Young, Corporal Willis A. Gunlikson, Private 1st Class Delmer L. Bockholdt. *Not in picture:* Corporal David N. Beckwermert, Master Sergeant Edgar J. Conn, Private 1st Class Al Bolejack, Private 1st Class John P. Campbell, Sergeant 1st Class Alvin L. Latimer, Private Douglas L. Mentzer, Sergeant George W. Smith, Private 1st Class Jack Croom.

Looking at a globe of the world, three friends from college located the Japanese Island of Hokkaido. Left to right: First Lieutenant Denzil D. Garrison, Second Lieutenant Morgan W. Eddleman, and Second Lieutenant Joseph F. Rolette. They were on their last short leave before heading across the Pacific and on to Hokkaido before being sent to Korea. Garrison is wearing a short Eisenhower jacket with his uniform. The others are wearing the traditional "pinks and greens" dress uniform.

when the Korean War broke out. President Harry S. Truman spoke of it as a "police action," but as I was to find out in the months to come, it was a real war indeed.

I was a member of Oklahoma's 45th Infantry Division, the famed Thunderbirds that came home from Europe with a glittering combat record after service in Sicily, Italy, France, and Germany. The pre-war division contained units in Oklahoma, Colorado, and Arizona, but after the war the 45th was reorganized as an all-Oklahoma division. There was a fierce prairie pride in the Thunderbirds throughout Oklahoma. Most of its officers and men assumed it would be picked to be in the vanguard of the National Guard divisions, and it was. In 1950, most of the officers, and a great number of the enlisted men of the division were veterans of World War II. We would have been offended for the most part, if we had not been chosen to go. And go we did. On 1 September 1950 we entered federal service.

At the outset, the Korean War did not go well for the United States. A fanatical communist army, well equipped with Soviet materiel, sliced through the ill-prepared and equipped South Korean Army. It was immediately evident that South Korea was doomed unless we gave them our complete backing, with both men and material. General Douglas MacArthur, the Commander in the Far East, was ordered to send all help available to the South Koreans. The first assistance we rendered was in the air, where we committed all available support to the desperate South Koreans. Then the 24th Infantry Division, under-strength and under-trained, was sent from its occupation duties in Japan to face the communist onslaught in Korea. The 24th Division was decimated by the invading North Korean People's Army (NKPA), as it was called. Soon, it became evident that if we were to save Korea from the communists, a lot more had to be put into our effort.

All over the world, American military units were alerted, and began receiving recruits and draftees, who commenced training for what we were beginning to realize was a real war. The United Nations reacted also, and North Korea was branded as an aggressor nation. The United States and other free nations took on the task of attempting to beat back the naked aggression of North Korea, which was under the domination and direction of Kim Il Sung, a puppet of Joseph Stalin and the Soviet Bear.

Unfortunately, the American military had been allowed to deteriorate after World War II, and we just did not have sufficient strength left to take on the pugnacious North Koreans. At the direction of President Truman, four National Guard divisions were called to federal service—the 28th Infantry of Pennsylvania, the 43rd Infantry of New Jersey, the 40th Infantry of California, and Oklahoma's 45th Infantry. All of these units had numerous World War II veterans, and there were high expectations that they would perform with distinction.

At the time, I was just ready to start my senior year at the University of Oklahoma School of Law, but that was put on hold while I went off to another war. Thirteen of us were called up from our Law School, and only eleven of us made it back to finish our legal education. I suppose that was really a pretty favorable percentage, although I am sure that the two who did not make it back would have liked a second roll of the dice. As the French say, "C'est le Guerre!"

On 1 September 1950, the 45th Division started its trek to Camp Polk, Louisiana. Polk was a World War II training facility, established in the "Cajun" part of the Bayou State. It was a good place to train, down amongst the pine trees and sandy soil of southwestern Louisiana. The post itself had not been well maintained after the war, and our first difficulty lay in rehabilitating the buildings and barracks. I

The USNS *General Hugh J. Gaffey* (AP-121), which along with the USNS *General Weigel* (AP-119), transported the 45th Infantry Division from New Orleans, Louisiana, across the Pacific to Hokkaido, Japan. Originally named the Admiral W. L. Capps, the *Gaffey* was built in 1945 with a displacement of 17,833 tons and a speed of 19 knots. The *Gaffey* carried the division headquarters for the 45th Infantry Division as was not as crowded as the *Weigel,* on which the author embarked.

was a member of the Division Artillery Staff when we were called up, but on reaching Camp Polk I was quickly assigned to Battery B of the 171st Field Artillery Battalion. I had been through the Field Artillery School twice, once as an OCS student, and then after the war I spent one summer attending the Fort Sill school as a first lieutenant. All in all, I was a pretty proficient artilleryman, I guess. At any rate, I was assigned as the Battery Executive Officer of Battery B. I was to stay with that unit for the best part of the next two years.

Before I reported to Polk, I was given the job of closing the temporary quarters of the 45th Division Artillery in Norman. That put me about five days behind the rest of the 171st. When I reported to the Bachelor Officers Quarters, all the rooms were taken save one. I was surprised that such a seemingly adequate room was left unoccupied, and I counted my blessings to have been able to move into it. I quickly threw in my luggage, and walked over to my new assignment at Battery B. That night, after dark, I finally dropped wearily on my bunk. As I gazed upward, I was astounded to see stars in the ceiling of my room. I jumped up and turned on the one light bulb hanging in the room. When I looked up there was a hole in the roof as big as a washtub. I now understood why no one had chosen that room before me. A heavy rain that night forced me to move my cot into the hall. It took another two weeks before the engineers came to plug that hole. Another demonstration of the military maxim learned by all soldiers, sooner or later: "If you want a decent deal, you had better see to it that you are first in line." I was an old enough soldier that I understood and I should have had someone pick out a room for me in my absence. Being new to the outfit, I just did not have anyone to look out for me. I would remedy that in the future.

As I began to perform my duties with the battery, I was pleasantly surprised to learn that most of the non-commissioned officers were veterans. As a matter of fact, the first sergeant, John T. Dunn, had been with the battery as first sergeant throughout World War II, in Sicily, Italy, France, and Germany. This was an outstanding plus. Eventually, Dunn turned out to be one of the closest friends I ever had in the world. Together, we built a superb artillery battery, which gave a good account of itself in Korea. But later I will tell more about John Dunn, and his brother, Jimmy, who was a section sergeant in the battery.

The unit was at about 55 percent strength when it reached Camp Polk. Camp Polk, now designated Fort Polk, is now a permanent post of the Regular Army, and the home of the Joint Readiness Training Center. That was not surprising, because it is a wonderful place to train combat soldiers. We eagerly awaited the arrival of our "fillers" as they were called, which were due soon from the replacement depots. We got them in two segments. First, 59 draftees from South Dakota, North Dakota, Nebraska, Oregon, and Washington State arrived. They were wonderful examples of the best America had. They were mostly farm boys, who made great soldiers when properly trained. That was our job. The names of those young soldiers showed many of them to be Swedes, Germans, Norwegians, and Danes. Hardy and healthy, they quickly developed into soldiers. I am sure most of them became good citizens after returning to civilian life.

The final draft of 19 fillers came just before we left Camp Polk for the Far East. They were different. They all came from Jersey City or thereabouts, and were mostly Italian and Irish. Their "Yankee" accents set them apart, and were more difficult to integrate into the battery. That was not really fair, because many of those easterners turned into excellent soldiers in spite of the fact that most of them, not all of them, talked too much. As it turned out, my driver in Korea was one of those "Yankees," Private Nicholas B. O'Reilly of Providence, Rhode Island. He was an excellent driver and soldier.

After strenuous basic training at Polk, we received our overseas orders in March of 1951. There was a bit of a crisis over in Hokkaido, the northern island of Japan. It seems that five Soviet airborne divisions were stationed on the coast of Siberia, only about 10 minutes flying time from Hokkaido, threatening to invade that island. We had to be sent over there, and quickly. To send us from the West Coast would have cost an extra month. We would have had to load up for rail transport and that was no easy task. Then unload in California and reload for sea transport. This brought about one of the wisest decisions ever made by the military. They decided to ship us out from New Orleans, Louisiana, by water, and send us through the Panama Canal. It saved one month of travel time, and may possibly have helped stave off a third world war because the Soviet airborne divisions were never parachuted onto Japanese soil. Maybe Stalin thought better of it because we had at least one combat outfit on Hokkaido, after we landed. We will probably never know the truth of that situation. But to be sure, Stalin was a cruel and tough customer.

Prior to shipment overseas, our unit had to go under overhead artillery fire at close range. This was supposed to familiarize the soldiers to the sound and feel of artillery as it passed over them. I was given the job of acting battery executive officer of a composite battery drawn from all the light artillery battalions in the division. This was not an easy task, and I feared that some cannoneer might cut the wrong powder charge, or some gunner might set the wrong data on the howitzer causing havoc among the soldiers out in front of the guns. Such was not the case, however, and the entire division passed under fire in a short time. I was pleased to have that job behind me.

Already the division was settling down into the formations that would work together in the trials ahead of it. In the division there were three infantry regiments and four artillery battalions. Three of the artillery battalions were armed with 105-mm. howitzers, designated as light artillery. The fourth battalion was armed with 155-mm. howitzers, designated as medium artillery. Each light battalion was in direct support of one of the infantry regiments, and the medium battalion was in general support of the entire division sector. In the 45th Division, the three infantry regiments were the 179th, the 180th and the 279th. The three light artillery battalions were the 158th, the 160th, and the 171st. The medium battalion was the 189th. The division was divided into three combat teams, consisting of one infantry regiment and one light artillery battalion, and attached service troops as needed. The 179th Infantry was teamed with the 158th Field Artillery Battalion. The 180th Infantry was teamed with the 171st Field Artillery Battalion, and the 279th Infantry was teamed with the 160th Field Artillery Battalion. Soon, much comradeship developed between each infantry regiment and its supporting field artillery battalion. Each team was designated as a "combat team," bearing the number of the infantry regiment involved. This system allowed much flexibility in the use of a division, or parts of a division, and proved to be a superior operational technique throughout World War II and in Korea. We were learning to work in such a system.

William R. Sumter, my old friend from college, was a second lieutenant in the battalion. He and I met two very attractive sisters who were attending Sophie Newcombe College for women in New Orleans. They came down to the dock to wish us bon-voyage. They looked so small and attractive down on the dock. They waved and blew us kisses, making us objects of envy to the thousands of GIs aboard. We felt superior in every way just then. When I reached Japan, the mail had collected for me during the voyage. Among the letters was a "Dear John" from my Sophie Newcomb friend, announcing that she had become engaged to a Louisianan. Sumter really kidded me about that, but in just two weeks he got an identical letter from the other sister. Such are the trials and tribulations of young bachelors going off to war. I cannot even remember their full names now.

I fell in love with the beautiful Caribbean Sea on the way to Panama. I have never been back since that trip, but I often think of the dark inky-blue waters there and long to go back. Maybe I can... after all I am only 76 years old now! We will see. But we were loaded on the USS *General Weigel,* a large troop transport, and the rest of the shipment was loaded on another General Class ship, the USNS *General Hugh J. Gaffey.* As usual, ours had more than twice as many men on it than did the other ship, which had the division headquarters aboard. That always seemed to be the way things turned out. Gazing at the other ship, which followed us through the Panama Canal, we thought it looked like heaven in comparison to the overcrowded *Weigel.*

Our latest fillers were left in Camp Polk to finish their basic training, and were to join us a few months later in Hokkaido. They were the Jersey City bunch, and a few of them gave us trouble for a long time. In all fairness I should mention that Private David Beckwermert, of Patterson, New Jersey, had the highest intelligence in the Battery, including that of the Battery Executive Officer, namely me! I am sure he made his mark on life after his service.

CHAPTER 2

THE PANAMA CANAL

After a three-day trip through the beautiful Caribbean Sea, we reached the Panama Canal. I shall never forget that journey from one of the world's great oceans, to the greatest of the world's oceans. The engineering feats of the builders of the canal were unbelievable, and we took pride in thinking that it was an American achievement. Our huge troopship edged its way through the locks and lakes, and we passed close to a British merchant ship that was pulled into a "parking," where ships waited as others passed, at the side of the canal. Our GIs began to call to the British crewmen, and slowly the contact became hostile. Some GI threw an old combat boot at an English merchant sailor down on the deck of the cargo ship, and the sailor ran into the interior of the ship. When he returned, he had painted a hammer-and-sickle, in the classic communist manner, on a large bucket. He yelled up to the GIs, "You blokes just wyte 'til old Joe Stalin gets ahold of you." After I pondered for awhile, it struck me as being not at all funny. I wondered if the Soviets were really just waiting for us, and how about that "Limey" seaman, supposedly our ally. Did he really want us to run afoul of Old Joe Stalin? In discussions after we passed through the canal, I found that some others were also thinking a lot about that scene.

We docked on the Pacific side of the canal, and the infantry soldiers were allowed off the ship to attend the local enlisted men's club. However, our artillery commanders decreed that we had to stay aboard the steaming troopship and gaze off into the lush tropics of Panama. I was really upset at this, because my uncle, Colonel William C. Garrison, was stationed there in Panama as the G-1 in charge of personnel of the Panama Base. I wanted to see him and his wife and three little girls, who were among my favorite cousins. I went down to the lower deck, and, sure enough there was my uncle waiting for me. I called out to him, and he came to the water's edge. He motioned for me to come ashore, and I called, "I can't, they won't let anyone off unless he has a tie on." Supposedly this was done to denote those who had official business ashore. We knew it to be a sham whereby only the chosen few could get on land. My uncle just took off his necktie, tied it in a large knot, and threw it over to me. I put the tie on and quickly went to the gangplank and marched ashore. We had a fine visit, and after I had seen my aunt and my cousins, my uncle and his friend, the Provost Marshall of the Panama Base Command, showed me Panama City. Suffice it to say, we saw plenty. I will not say more now on that subject, but it remained a source of laughter between my uncle and

The author, First Lieutenant Denzil D. Garrison, aboard the U.S.N.S. *General William Weigel*, passing through Lake Gatun in the Panama Canal. The voyage from New Orleans, Louisiana, to the Panama Canal took 3 days. The long voyage across the Pacific, via. San Francisco, California, took 30 days, with an unscheduled stop on the West Coast to offload four seriously ill soldiers.

me for many years. In later years he became a major general, and Inspector General of the United States Army, but he still laughed about how he got me off the troopship and into some of the most notorious nightspots in Panama.

I was not too popular for a few days with my buddies who stayed on board. However, when I described how it all came to pass, and all the things I had seen, they were glad someone got to see what they believed we all should have seen. We left hot humid Panama and traveled several days right along the equator. Even our khaki clothing felt like heavy wool. Would we ever be cool again? For that, we just had to wait a few days.

We sailed along the equator a fortnight, and then turned north. Originally, we were to go directly to Hokkaido, but a very scary thing happened. Four soldiers became very ill with spinal meningitis, a dangerous disease and very contagious on a crowded troopship loaded to capacity. The decision was made to land at San Francisco, California, to leave those sick soldiers in the hospital there. Today, this would have probably been done by helicopter, but the technology at that time was not quite that advanced. We pulled into the dock at San Francisco and spent three days there; replenishing supplies and doing those things the Navy had to do, in its strange ways. During the stay in California, none of the troops were allowed off the ship. It was fascinating to see how the GIs managed to get ashore for one last fling. Two outstanding examples of GI craftiness stick in my memory.

The first was the great "Egg Crate Caper." A conveyor roller went from the ship's galley to the dock. I noticed that a number of empty egg crates were being off-loaded. These were large crates, supposedly filled with cartons to hold eggs. Finally, one military police trooper (MP), stationed on the dock to keep the GIs aboard stopped the conveyor. He opened a large crate, and there were more than just eggs inside. About every third crate contained a very live GI, determined on taking in the scenes and adventures of San Francisco. I suppose I should have been offended by their machinations, but I really envied their ingenuity and hoped that some of them made it to town. Based on certain medical treatment that about 10 of them received after we

had again put to sea, it was obvious that at least a few of them were successful in getting off the ship.

Then there was the second great "Garbage Can Caper." This one was witnessed by hundreds of soldiers who were amused onlookers. There was a gangplank from the galley to the shore, and the GIs who were serving as kitchen police (KP) were given the duty, from time to time, of taking out large garbage cans to the dock and emptying them in a container brought up for that purpose. One particular busy pair carried a large can onto the dock and started to walk toward the entryway to the town. The MPs, by now much wiser, blew their shrill whistles and swooped down on the can and its innocent-appearing carriers. When the MPs took the lid off the can there was a very chagrined GI who was marched back aboard to do an extra day's duty as KP. As one fellow said as they were taking the "culprit" back aboard, "He'd better watch out, or he'll get sent to Korea." That was the way we all felt. What could they do to us that was not going to be done anyway!

On the left is the author, First Lieutenant Denzil D. Garrison and on the right is his friend First Lieutenant Bailey Wilbanks Harrison of Wewoka, Oklahoma. When the photograph was taken, the U.S.N.S. *General William Weigel* was sailing near the equator in the Pacific after clearing the Panama Canal. Like all aboard ship who had never before crossed the equator, Garrison and Wilbanks were initiated in the rite of passage to the court of King Neptune. The warm weather soon turned cold as the ship headed into the North Pacific.

Everything wasn't all that funny about those hours we spent aboard ship looking out into San Francisco. These were young men in the prime of their lives, many of whom had left new wives and young babies at home. That was not an easy thing for those soldiers to face. Looking out on the dock, there were dozens of telephone booths in plain sight. Those poor guys saw what was their last chance to talk to their wives and families for a long time, maybe forever, only a few feet down that dock. It was too much for one of our sergeants to handle. Sergeant Alvin L. Latimer did a very foolish, but understandable thing. He jumped to the dock from the deck of the ship, breaking both of his feet in the process. The guards crowded around him, and the medics were called to the scene. Brigadier General Hal L. Muldrow, Jr., the division artillery commander, was

Like most other Thunderbirds, First Lieutenant Denzil D. Garrison, of the 171st Field Artillery Battalion, was glad to land on Hokkaido and began training for service in Korea. Note the pup tent in the left background. After the crowded conditions on the troop ships during the long voyage across the Pacific, living in the field on Hokkaido was a welcome change; however, once Battery B reached Hokkaido the morale of the men rapidly improved.

summoned. Latimer was in a state of shame for what he had done, but Muldrow told him, "Don't worry son, you get well, and we'll be glad to have you back when you're mended. You are a good soldier." Latimer was taken off the dock on a stretcher, crying real tears when he looked up on deck to see his comrades still aboard. He was an American Indian, and strikingly handsome. He had served in the Navy in World War II, and he was a real loss to us. Latimer joined us again about three months later, in Japan. He went to Korea with us, and gave a good account of himself while there. He joined the Regular Army after the Korean War, and did three tours in Vietnam before his health broke and he died in a veteran's home. He was in his own way a "good soldier" as Brigadier General Muldrow had said. His service in three of his country's wars proved that. Muldrow also was an American Indian.

So we left San Francisco, passing under a very beautiful Golden Gate Bridge, most of us wondering if we would ever see it again. Most of us did, but too darn many did not.

By now, the weather had cooled a lot. We turned to the northwest as we cleared the harbor and headed into the stormy North Pacific Ocean. Before long, we wondered how they had ever seen fit to name that ocean "the Pacific Ocean." It rained, and then it rained some more. The waves became monstrous, and we saw the full fury of a Pacific storm. Many of the men became seasick, and it was pretty uncomfortable for us all. Finally, we passed out of the storm and into the cold reaches of the North Pacific. We had worn our khaki uniforms in the tropics, and we could not reach our baggage in the ship's hold to get our warmer clothes. Most of us were smart enough at least to save out a field jacket. I was one of those who had a jacket, and I was glad. The cold, bleak North Pacific made a lasting impression on all the young soldiers on that great gray troopship. We shivered and wondered what would be our fate.

The crowded conditions of a troopship are indescribable. Bunks four deep, which are little more than thin canvas strips, attached to the bulkhead of the troopship. More than at any other time the accommodations of the enlisted men were far inferior to the accommodations for the officers. The men had to be fed their two meals a day while standing in a spare mess that had no provision for making the meal palatable. Morale on a troopship begins to disintegrate after three or four days, and that was a worry to me. My first sergeant came to me about half way across and told me that one of our men, named Bardwell, was seriously ill in the troop compartment from a severely infected tooth. He had a hard time making it past the guards to find me, but he was determined and obviously knew what he was about. The Navy was much more restrictive in separating officers and enlisted men than was the Army. But, I saw him arguing with the guard and quickly went to him. He explained the situation to me, and we went below at once. There was poor Bardwell, with his head swollen twice it's normal size, in intense pain. I could see he was feverish, and very sick. I went up to the sick bay and found the Navy dental assistant. At first he refused to even see Bardwell, but I insisted. Finally, the first sergeant brought him to the sick bay, and the dentist's assistant saw we had a sick man, indeed. He called for the ship's dentist, who took one look at Bardwell and put him in the sick bay at once. The offending molar was extracted, and the patient was filled with penicillin, which killed the infection by the time we landed. I do not doubt that the treatment saved that soldier's life. It took several days ashore to bring back the discipline that had been lost during that cramped and uncomfortable trip. I hoped we would never have another like it.

We were told that we were headed to Hokkaido, the northern island of the Japanese homeland. Hokkaido had not been made a part of Japan proper until 1876. For a lot of reasons it was described as the Alaska of Japan. We expected it to be cold, and we were not wrong in that regard. We expected it to be primitive, but we were agreeably surprised to find that parts of the island were quite advanced by Japanese standards.

We discussed among ourselves the aboriginal people of Hokkaido known as the Ainu race. For those of us from Oklahoma, they sounded something like our Indians back home. We could hardly wait to see that culture, which we later observed first-hand many times.

CHAPTER 3

HOME IN HOKKAIDO

Finally, 30 days after leaving New Orleans, we sighted the Japanese island of Hokkaido. We sailed up the Tsugaru Strait past Hakodate, a fairly large town with an imposing Christian convent high on a hill, on into Uchiura Bay to the port of Muroran. We were the first American troops ever to land there, and we were not surprised to see that World War II naval bombardment of the steel and paper mills had left marks that were still evident. We were told to disembark into waiting trucks, which we did. This landing was the fifth amphibious landing made by the 45th Infantry Division and the first ever made without hostile enemy fire. We were somber as we were driven to Chitose. There we found a macadam airfield that had been used by the Japanese Navy during the war. As a matter of fact, the pilots who bombed Pearl Harbor had trained there. We later learned that the Pearl Harbor attack force had gathered at Hokkaido, and had left their fog-shrouded seaports in secret to deliver the bombs at Pearl Harbor bringing America into World War II.

The first dawn in our primitive camp brought a squadron of Soviet Mig fighter planes overhead. They did not shoot, but they buzzed the hell out of us. That was very disconcerting, to say the least. The second dawn brought the Migs back, but that day they were intercepted by a squadron of Air Force F-86 Saber Jet fighters that chased the Migs back to Siberia. Never again did the Soviet planes come back. Whether the F-86s shot them down, we did not know. It was

The Thunderbirds of Tent Four in front of their quarters on Hokkaido. Front row, left to right: Corporal James McLeod, Private Morton Nosenchuk, Sergeant Walter V. Allison, Sergeant Jesse C. McGee, and Sergeant James L. Steidley. Second row, left to right Corporal Lawrence A. Mack and Sergeant Donald J. Stacey. Hokkaido had been used by the Japanese Army as a training area during World War II and the Japanese planned to make their last stand on the island. The Thunderbirds, as the Oklahoma guardsmen were known, also found the island an excellent place to train.

comforting to know that the Air Force was watching over us. Chitose was five minutes flying time by jet fighter from the Soviet airfields in Siberia. That gave us something to think about.

We were placed in a camp of large squad tents near the airport at Chitose. The other regiments had better quarters near the large city of Sapporo, but we were satisfied with our spot. We worked hard to establish the encampment, and soon a disciplined military post emerged. We were in the most strategic spot on the island, next to the airstrip. If the Soviet airborne divisions came, they would try to capture the airfield first. We had to prevent that, if we could. We really knew that there probably was no way that one infantry division could stand against five airborne divisions, but we were going to give it a hell of a try if the occasion arose.

Our own particular squad tent became rather famous. We went into the little town of Chitose and purchased a ready-made house front from the equivalent of a Japanese lumberyard. The Japanese built very portable houses, and one could buy parts of a building, of very light flimsy construction, and just tack it together to make a house by Japanese standards. We purchased the front of such a house with windows and a door, and tacked our tent around it. It made a half-tent "house" that became the envy of all the other tent dwellers. It was bright and airy inside our tent, and people came to visit us often just to see our tent. All six officers of the battery lived there, including my commanding officer, Captain Al Norman, who was a good soldier and a good commander. He was a veteran of World War II, as were all the other officers of the battery. It was his idea to put the house front on our tent, making it the showplace of the camp. It showed like a lantern. We held our breath because we were afraid someone would force us to take down our masterpiece, but no one did.

We immediately began to train harder than any of us had ever trained before. We were isolated in a cold and hostile place, and we had all the training ground we needed to really become hard and ready for what we knew was ahead. The quality of our troops was outstanding, and they quickly became proficient soldiers. Morale was very good, under the circumstances, and we all developed into trained soldiers accustomed to living in the field. Our training paid off when we went on into Korea, several months later. My battery became a model of proficiency in delivering artillery fire for the infantry we supported. We thought we were the best, and we were not too far from wrong in that regard.

The Japanese had completed extensive fortification of Hokkaido during World War II. The Japanese Emperor had planned to make his last stand up there, if the war had not ended as it did. The key to the defense of the island was the Ishikari Plain, which ran right down the center. We found an astonishing fortified range of hills running down the west edge of the plain that contained a system of tunnels, all connected, with firing positions for artillery along its 40-mile length. The main road of the island ran along the base of the hills. We shuddered to think how many men we would have lost, if we had been forced to dig those Japanese out of the center of Hokkaido. It made us thankful that the atomic bomb was used to end the war. Many of us would have given our lives taking the redoubt of Hokkaido, if the war had continued.

In our training, we came to know the Ainu, a people who had inhabited the island centuries before the Japanese conquered it. At one time the Ainu inhabited a large part of the Japanese home islands but were driven out of the southern islands by the Japanese who arrived from China. The Ainu had much more hair on their faces than did the Japanese and they were a larger race, man for man. They are a separate racial strain, and have been described as semi-Caucasian. I really do not know about that, but I found them to be very interesting.

Their religion was based on the worship of bears which were native to the island. The heroes of the Ainu race entered into individual combat with a caged bear, fighting without weapons. By the time we got there, it had deteriorated to the point that five or six Ainus entered a bear cage with clubs, and dispatched the poor bear in short order—so much for the Ainu heroes.

First Lieutenant Denzil D. Garrison standing before the famous "house tent" the officers of Battery B, 171st Field Artillery Battalion constructed on Hokkaido. The windowpanes were designed by the Japanese to use in their homes. The walls were built separately and then joined later. Garrison and the other members of the tent purchased the pre-built section to make a ready-made house front for the squad tent.

It was fascinating to watch Ainu artisans make carved bears, which were recognized as their trademark. They used both their hands and feet while carving. The bears they made became popular to us, and we all had at least one of them. They sold for one dollar, and if the bear was carrying a fish, as some of the fancy ones were, it would cost a dollar and a quarter. I still have two of those bears that have become very valuable through the years.

The more primitive Ainu villages were known only to us, and many had never seen white men until we came. Many of Ainus existed through the sale of charcoal, which they were very adept at making. Very soon they became addicted to chewing gum and American cigarettes.

It was on Hokkaido that First Sergeant John Dunn first amazed me. John was a very complex man in many ways. He was a Choctaw Indian and though not well educated in the classical sense, John possessed much native intelligence. While on Hokkaido John came to me and said that he had studied the Japanese language a bit since our arrival. He said that he was astounded to find that many of the words of the Japanese language meant the same thing in Choctaw. John had a list of about 20 words of Japanese written on a paper. He then listed the same 20 words, but in Choctaw. Then he listed the English translation of both. I was fascinated to see the comparison, and more fascinated yet that John Dunn had taken the time or made the effort to meticulously list those words. I have always wondered if those interchangeable words were only coincidences, or had John hit upon something profound. I will have to leave that for someone else to figure out, but it is an interesting thing to contemplate.

Intelligence sources reported to us that the Soviets were planning to strike Hokkaido in an airborne attack on the first of May in 1951. We knew that we were close to a third world war at that time, and were not surprised when they took all the artillery firing units of the division, and placed them in firing position around the airfield. We dug all sorts of fortifications in the volcanic ash of Hokkaido, and we became as ready as we could for whatever came. After about 20 days under full combat load, the crisis passed, and we went back to our tent city. I worked with Sergeant Walter Allison, who was the brains of my battery fire direction center (FDC), to construct a deep and safe dugout for the battery command post (CP). I really liked and respected Walter, who, in later years, became president of the largest bank in my hometown. It was easy to spot him as a "comer." In the end, we constructed a model dugout, just in time to abandon it when we moved back to our tent city. That dugout is probably still waiting for someone.

One of the funniest things of my service took place when we got back to the airfield at Chitose. Second Lieutenant Bill Sumter rode back with me in my jeep, sucking on a bottle of bourbon all the way. We were relieved to be through with our stay in bunkers, and we relished the thought of taking a warm shower and having a hot meal. Sumter prevailed on me to go by the officer's club, situated at the airfield, for a little celebration of our homecoming. We entered the club noisily, and walked by the hat check counter.

Leaning across the counter was an Air Force officer talking on the telephone. As he passed the counter, Sumter just could not resist the temptation. He reached out and "goosed" that airman, who was as yet unidentified. As the airman turned and revealed his gray hair, I knew we were in trouble. He was angry, and he wore the eagles of a full colonel. We both snapped to attention, and the colonel said to Sumter, "Lieutenant, when I was a second lieutenant, I wouldn't even goose a first lieutenant, much less an Airbase Commander!" He was livid. I could not suppress a laugh, and he turned to me and ordered me to attention. I quickly froze, as did Sumter, who stood not too steadily, trying to look military.

The colonel spoke into the telephone and told his listener that he had just been goosed by a drunk Army second lieutenant. He said the lieutenant would remember this day for a long time. All the while, we stood at attention.

The colonel hung up the telephone, and just drummed his fingers on the counter, looking down and obviously thinking about what he was getting ready to say. Finally, he stood up and turned to the unsteady Sumter, still trying to look military. "I don't know what the hell you think you are doing, but you won't get away with actions like that," said the colonel. He then proceeded to give Sumter a real "ass-chewing," as we called it in the military. Finally, Sumter blurted, "May I say something, sir?" The colonel said, "What in the hell do you have to say?" Sumter, still at attention, said, "Sir, I think you are a hell of a nice fellow!" The colonel bit his lip, and, thinking, finally said, "Oh what the hell. Come on in and I'll buy you a drink." They went to the bar, and shared not one, but several drinks. I can still see them as the club closed, patting one another on the back, and exclaiming about their new friendship. I thought I had seen it all. That encounter became famous in our outfit.

About this time, I was made Battery Commander of Battery B. Captain Norman was moved to the Division Artillery staff, and I took over the reins. That was a proud day for me, and I hoped I would not be found wanting in the months to come. We continued to train, and passed our battery tests given by the Army to assure that we were ready for combat. So did the other batteries of the battalion. We were ready and it came as no surprise that we were alerted for movement to Korea in November of 1951.

A good example of Japanese folk art is this hand-carved driver, oxen, and cart made by a local Japanese artist on Hokkaido. It depicts a Japanese ox-driver and a "honey wagon," which was used, and probably still is, to gather and transport raw human sewage to farmers' fields. As you can guess, that was a smelly venture. This little carving cost $2.75 at the post exchange in Chitose. Quite a bargain!

These two carved bears were made in 1951 by an Ainu artisan on Hokkaido. The artisan used both his hands and feet in carving these figures. His feet held the block he was carving from, and skillfully turned the figure as needed. He carved by hand, using a very sharp steel knife. No machinery of any kind was used. The bears are pictured carrying stolen fish on their backs. Evidently the bears did this often when they raided Ainu fishing villages. The bears were considered sacred by the Ainus, as part of their animist religious, especially in times past. These expensive carvings cost $1.25 each at the post exchange!

Just before we left Chitose my First Sergeant John Dunn and his brother Sergeant Jimmy Dunn were in town at what we called a "beer hall." As a matter of fact, that is what the Japanese called them. Japanese beer, by the way, is excellent as far as beer goes. There was a quartermaster laundry unit at Chitose made up of black soldiers. Somehow, the two Dunn boys, who were Choctaw Indians, became involved in a one-sided conflict with a room full of "laundrymen," and Jimmy Dunn was badly hurt by a broken beer bottle which was used to carve up his scalp "pretty good" as his brother described it. Many stitches were required to suture the wounds. John fought a delaying action long enough to get Jimmy out of the hall and into the hospital. He had some superficial wounds himself. When he came to report the incident to me he said one particular fellow had started and fomented it all, and he described him in detail. He was the one who cut up Jimmy with the broken beer bottle. John said he would take care of that fellow in good time, and I was quite sure he would if ever the opportunity arose.

Just before we left for Korea, John Dunn came to me and said, "Lieutenant, I have something to tell you. I went to that big stack of cordwood out at the main gate, and waited there the biggest part of the night for that guy to come by who cut up my brother. Finally, just before dawn, he stumbled by. I made sure he was the right guy, and he was. I took one of those sticks of cordwood and hit him in the head as hard as I could. He went down and didn't move, and I came home. I don't know if he is living or dead."

I was flabbergasted. I just did not know what to do. Here was my best, most decorated soldier, the ranking non-commissioned officer in the battalion in danger of being lost to the country and us. I called the MP officer there on the post and asked him if he had received any reports of assaults involving soldiers. He said none had been reported, but that he would let me know if any such reports came in. Good!

The first and only vehicles we were allowed to take to Korea were our kitchen trucks. We loaded ours onto a Landing Ship Tank (LST), and we were to send five men with each truck, to have meals ready for the troops when they arrived in Korea. I thought, "Why don't I just send First Sergeant Dunn to Korea with the kitchen truck?" The LST was waiting to leave, and we were ordered to send the five-man detachment to travel with the kitchen at once. The five men left, and First Sergeant Dunn was one of them. We never heard of the incident ever again. I have always wondered what happened to that soldier who was cracked with a stick of cordwood. Hopefully, it was no more than a bad headache. At any rate, I have always hoped that was the case in this instance.

This solution was worked out by our very astute unit administrator, Warrant Officer Ernest T. McKean, who was invaluable to me both as a "keeper of the records," and as one of the best friends I ever had. He saved my career a hundred times, because I was not the best at "paper work" in those days. I kept frequent contact with Ernest after the war. He had been an infantryman in Europe in World War II, and he had two stepbrothers who were officers in the division, as well as a brother who was an enlisted man in the 180th Infantry Regiment. They all made it home, thank God.

CHAPTER 4

FROZEN CHOSEN

We were told that we were to relieve the First Cavalry Division, a Regular Army outfit that had been in Korea a long time. The First Cav, as we called it, had been "rotated" down to the bone. By that I mean that practically none of the original members of the division were left with it. Gradually, the combat effectiveness of the unit had deteriorated. They were ready for relief. One catch was that we were to trade equipment with the First Cavalry Division, including all of our artillery pieces and rolling stock. Our equipment left on Hokkaido was in excellent condition. The equipment left to us in Korea was in very sad shape. We more or less expected this, but the enormity of the problem was more than we ever contemplated. Thank God we did not have to fight any big battles before we had some time to get the howitzers in firing condition and to get our trucks and vehicles in operable shape. After about 90 days in the line, we had the equipment up in very usable shape. Our troops were outstanding in getting this done.

We loaded on trucks in Chitose and Sapporo, and headed back to Muroran, the port where we had disembarked eight months earlier. I thought our men looked resolute and well trained, which they were. Our Regimental Combat Team loaded on the USS *Pickaway*, an assault personnel carrier, which was a veteran of Pacific fighting in World War II and Korea. A small officer's wardroom was available to us for the three-day trip to Inchon, on the west coast of Korea, where we were to

171
B

disembark in landing craft. Inchon had one of the greatest tides in the world, and our arrival had to be gauged to a time when the tide was "in."

I noticed a young infantry lieutenant sitting alone in the wardroom, talking to no one. Shortly after nightfall on the next to last day of our trip, he got up and went out on deck alone. We heard a gunshot, and rushed out to see what it was. The lieutenant had shot himself in the head with his .45-caliber automatic pistol. That was shocking to us, and I will admit I was a bit unnerved by it. We all wondered why he did not wait and take some of the enemy with him. He was not thinking rationally when he ended it all.

We landed after dark on 7 December 1951, by landing boats that were pulled up next to the Pickaway. We loaded into the boats by crawling down scramble nets put over the side of the ship. Those nets were difficult, to say the least, and a bobbing landing boat could be deadly if it took a dive just before a soldier stepped into it. But, happily, we had no serious injuries in loading. We landed on the beach at Inchon in bitterly cold weather. As I remember, it was below five degrees that night. The wind whipped icy shards into our skin, and we were chilled to the bone. The cold is what the Korean veterans remember above all else. Hanging off of Siberia, the Korean Peninsula has some of the most severe weather ever faced by American combat troops. We were expecting this, but the shock of standing out in that kind of weather struck us full blast. We knew we had some hard days ahead.

Corporal John P. Campbell, Jr., of Salem, Oregon, on Hokkaido standing beside the metal guidon of Battery B, 171st Field Artillery. When ordered to Korea, the guidon was one of the few pieces of equipment that the battery took to Korea. Most vehicles and other equipment were left in Japan because the battery was supposed to take over the equipment left in Korea by the First Cavalry Division that was rotating home. Unfortunately the equipment left behind by the First Cavalry was sometimes worthless.

The first position occupied by Battery B, 171st Field Artillery near Chorwon when the unit arrived in Korea. The battery stayed in this position for several months before it moved to another sector of the frontlines. Note the path leading up the hill in the center of the photograph. This path was used to man and maintain a heavy machine gun position on top of the hill. Note the two tents in the right background that are surrounded by revetments constructed from empty ammunition boxes that have been filled with dirt and stacked.

The view of the enemy frontlines from Battery B's observation post on Hill 347. Although a part of Battery B, the unit's artillery observers spent most of their time with frontline infantry units so that they could call in supporting artillery fire on enemy troops. It was dangerous duty. Notice the path in the foreground. Should one slip it was a sheer drop down the mountainside.

First Lieutenant Edward Saunders, a forward observer for Battery B, peering across no man's land toward enemy positions from an observation post on the frontlines. Note the tremendous destruction caused by artillery fire on the hilltop and the absence of tree branches. A telephone line connecting the sandbagged bunker on the left of the photograph with the fire direction center can be seen running along the ground. The telephone line allowed Saunders to call in fire missions to the battalion fire direction center.

Standing on the left is Master Sergeant James A. Nolan. On the right is Sergeant First Class John L. Cloyd. Both men were from McAlester, Oklahoma. Note the deep snow of the Korean winter. Cloyd was fortunate to be wearing overshoes.

Empty shell casings and surplus powder bags fill a howitzer pit after a long night of fighting. This is the refuse from one howitzer firing for one night. The crew members obviously are resting as their steel helmets are hanging on the parapet. A night of such fighting was exhausting to a gun crew. Notice the bricks placed in the bottom of the gun pit to keep the weapon and its crew out of the mud.

A desolate Korean mountainside on that portion of the frontlines covered by Battery B. Note the effects of hundred of rounds of artillery fire and aerial bombardment that destroyed practically all vegetation. When the rains started the absence of vegetation turned the mountainside to mud making climbing difficult. Note the winding path leading to the top of the mountain.

One of the best soldiers of them all was Warrant Officer Ernest T. McKean of McAlester, Oklahoma. The Japanese word for warrant officer was "Juni." Consequently McKean became known as "Juni" to his comrades. He was beloved by all and a close friend of the author until the day he died.

A 105-mm. howitzer of Battery B has just fired a round, as have the other weapons of the battery. Note the smoke coming from the three other guns in the photograph. All six guns of the battery are firing for effect in support of the infantry. The terrific blast of the artillery pieces has caused a blurred image. The gunner, on the right of the piece, is holding a field telephone to his ear in order to receive fire commands from the fire direction center. He is ready to pull the lanyard that will fire the piece again. The cannoneer on the left holds a projectile ready to load. This action took place on January 19, 1952.

Standing not far from where we disembarked from the landing boats was a Korean train with passenger cars attached. We marched over and entered the cars. We were disappointed to find that there were no panes of glass in the windows of the old cars, and neither were there any doors. The wind whipping through the cars was increased by the speed of the train when we started moving north. Our feet felt as though they were frozen in blocks of ice, and our faces became numb. It was one of the most miserable times of our lives. The old passenger cars had been third class to start with, and the rigors of war had left them in shambles. I am sure that those old cars had moved Republic of Korea (ROK) soldiers, and in all probability enemy soldiers up and down the peninsula. There were no stoves on the cars, and absolutely nothing to keep the wind out. I had a bottle of scotch whiskey in my bag, which I passed around to help make the icy cold a little more bearable.

No one had any idea where the train was taking us. We discussed among ourselves what our destination might be, and decided that we must be going to a staging area where we would stay for a few days before going into combat. How mistaken we were. We traveled for hours to the north, and finally stopped at some sort of railhead. We gingerly hopped off the old train on half frozen feet that hurt as we walked to waiting trucks. I noticed shell flashes on the horizon, and I knew that the front was in that direction.

We loaded into the trucks and started toward the flashes that were growing closer with each turn of the wheels. Finally we turned up a smaller road and went several hundred yards, when off to our right, a six-gun battery of 105-mm. howitzers fired. We realized that we were in a battery position. The trucks stopped and we were unloaded. We were marched to a kitchen tent, and there was our own mess, set up and waiting. Huge pots of black coffee warmed us up, and we were happy to see our five men, including the First Sergeant who had come with the kitchen truck. I was happy to tell John Dunn that we had heard nothing about the incident at the gate in Chitose.

We were in the battery area of Battery B, 77th Field Artillery Battalion, First Cavalry Division. We were told by Captain James

Lynch, the commander of the unit that we were the first artillery battery of the 45th Division to reach the front. Lynch was a splendid fellow, and was the star of the traveling "Jimmy Lynch Auto Show" before the war. He was glad to see us, and he personally took our gun crews to each gun in order to let his men show mine what they could about each piece. Rapport quickly was established between the two groups. Soon, my cannoneers were unloading ammunition boxes and preparing shells for firing.

Early the next morning, Captain Lynch took me down to the number one piece and installed our gun crew on the weapon. Soon, a fire mission came in over the telephone from the battalion fire direction center, and our soldiers handled the weapon. When it was ready to fire, I pulled the lanyard myself. In so far as I know, I fired the first round of the Korean War from the 45th Division Artillery.

About noon the next day our battalion commander arrived and announced that he was going to fire the first round of the war from the 45th Division Artillery. He had some chalk with which he wrote his name on the projectile, and he fired the shell into enemy lines. He always bragged that he fired the first shell, but my men and I knew he had not. We got quite a kick out of that. We liked our battalion commander all right, but it was sort of hard to really respect him due to his constant worrying about his commanders and what they might be thinking of him. He was short, fat and squat. We used to say that he was deathly afraid of "the brass" at division, the brass at Division Artillery, the brass of the infantry, and the Chinese Communist Army (CCA), and in that order! It was difficult to serve under such as that.

We stayed in the same battery area with the First Cav outfit for a week. Captain Lynch was helpful and friendly until the last. Our men got along fairly well together, but trouble began to show up in the last days of the First Cav's stay. One of our men came to me with the news that a shotgun that he had brought over was missing. I reported this to Captain Lynch, along with the opinion of the victim that one of the First Cav soldiers had stolen it. As the men of the First Cav were preparing to leave, Captain Lynch lined them up before our men. He announced that we suspected one of them had stolen the shotgun. He said, "If such is the case, the guilty person should make himself known by raising his hand." No one stirred. Captain Lynch then ordered each man of his command to empty his barracks bag right there and then. After mumbling and grumbling, the bags were emptied. One sergeant slowly emptied his bag, and there was the shotgun. Captain Lynch was livid, and cut the stripes off the uniform of the sergeant before the men of both batteries. He announced that the transgressor would be prosecuted after the unit reached Hokkaido. We never heard anything more about the matter. I often think of Captain Lynch to this very day, and my memories of him are positive.

We were situated about 3,500 yards behind the front in a mountain valley that opened toward the front. Our six howitzers were dug into the frozen earth about two feet, and sandbags were placed around the emplacements. Small ravines, leading in all directions, surrounded the battery area. A road ran in front of the howitzers, which was opposite from the teachings of the Artillery School. There we learned that the roadway into the battery area should be in the rear of the guns, not in front of it. The topography of the area dictated that the battery had to fire over the entry road. Under the circumstances we had no choice but to do it that way, although we tried to think of some way to do it differently after the position became ours. We soon became famous to anyone traveling down that road, because at any moment a fire mission might be called in and six screaming 105-mm. shells might go streaking over the road.

At first we tried to warn the traffic of the firing, but then we realized that it was not feasible. We just fired when we had to, and the worse thing that happened to travelers was a bad headache and a frightful experience. They soon learned that passing in front of Battery B was akin to "running the gauntlet."

There was a long valley that emptied into the front of the battery, from the direction of the battlefront. This valley worried me, because I feared that enemy infiltrators would use that natural passageway to enter our battery area. We placed two .50-caliber machine guns on either side of that valley, and gave orders for those posts to be occupied every night. There was barbed wire across the mouth of the valley, and we were told that trip flares and mines had been placed there by the First Cav. The first night we were there after the First Cav's battery left, we were understandably jittery. Special Service had sent us a projector and the film *An American in Paris.* I told the first sergeant to put the projector in the kitchen tent and to make the tent light proof and we would try to have a movie. I had brought a war surplus generator with me. We hooked up the generator and began to watch Leslie Caron and Gene Kelly dancing their way through Paris. We split showings so that about 30 men at a time could watch. It took about four hours for the first showing, due to the fact that the projector broke down 18 times. The cold weather made the film very brittle, and we just spliced our way through it! Never before or since had we seen such a film. Finally, we gave up and decided to wait for spring.

Shortly after the end of the film was reached we were shocked by the firing of one of the trip flares across our worrisome valley. Another one went flying up and lighted the area again. We could see some movement, and our machine guns opened up into the valley. After several bursts, I told them by telephone to cease-fire. We waited through the rest of the night on guard, but nothing more happened. We never knew who or what set off the trip flares, and we were puzzled that none of the mines were detonated. Many thought that some of the small deer that abounded in Korea had been the culprits, but none of them were found dead in the minefield. I personally thought that we were being infiltrated by line-crossers who were thwarted by the flares. At any rate, that proved to be our baptism of suspense in our Korean sojourn.

We were in direct support of our regular infantry regiment, the 180th. This regiment was a good one, probably one of the best. The 171st Field Artillery Battalion was the direct artillery support unit for the 180th Regimental Combat Team. We furnished forward observer (FO) teams to each company of the regiment. They lived with the infantry and called in fire missions when needed. Those were dangerous assignments, because the FO teams stayed where the action was hottest up front. The team was headed by a lieutenant, who commanded a party of four that included a driver, a wireman, and a forward observer sergeant. They were beloved by the infantry, who watched over them like hawks. Our infantry regiment arrived in Korea with us, and they were waiting for our observers when we took over from the First Cav. I sent our FO teams, including my good and close friend Sumter, up to the front. We had some losses among those teams, but, all in all, we had astounding luck in keeping them alive.

Soon after we went into combat, I decided to get up to see the front. My brother, a captain in the 179th Infantry, served with the infantry for many months during World War II. He cautioned me to stay out of harm's way, but I was filled with just enough courage to want to get up to the front on the slightest excuse. My driver, Nick O'Reilly, and I were commonly seen all over the front. Looking back, I can see that I had no business poking around up there, but just the same, I am glad I did. Most of the close calls I had in Korea happened when I was someplace snooping around where I had no business being. I talked to O'Reilly about those times not long ago. He still lives in Rhode Island, and he has retired from an automotive repair shop he owned. He learned what he knew about cars as a jeep driver in Korea, he says.

When I got up to the Main Line of Resistance (MLR) I did a lot of studying of the enemy situation. The division sector contained some features that became famous in the months to come. There is no doubt about it; we were placed in the hottest sector of the front. Starting on the left of the sector was what is known as "Old Baldy," correctly spoken of as Hill 255. Just to the right of Old Baldy was "Pork Chop Hill." Next were Hill 191 and its infamous "Point Eerie." Directly behind and a part of Hill 191, was a huge mass known as "T-bone Mountain."

These were forbidding places, that were hard to attack and easier to defend, occupied by the Chinese 42nd Army, which was made up mostly of large and sturdy Mongolians. Those fellows were barrel chested, stocky, and many of them were over six feet tall. They were tough hombres.

We came to know every inch of that bleak landscape like the backs of our hands. All of the brush and trees of these landmarks had long since been shot down, and it looked as though they would never again grow anything green and alive. I often wonder what it looks like now.

We needed to take some Chinese prisoners for intelligence purposes as soon as we could. We set up forward outposts for that purpose, mostly to no avail. One patrol brought in a huge Mongolian, badly wounded, but still alive. The patrol leader, a sergeant, turned him over to the S-2 Intelligence Officer. The poor Mongolian was so badly wounded that he died before any questions could be asked of him. The chagrined sergeant said to the S-2, "I'm sorry sir, I tried to just shoot him around the edges." We got no information from that source. That winter we tried to snag prisoners every day, but it was not easy. The Chinese were a long way away across the valley floor. We caused them plenty of casualties, but mostly with long-range weapons. Soon, that situation changed.

CHAPTER 5

OLD BALDY

We soon found that Old Baldy was a center of Chinese activity. Our air support came from several sources, but we particularly liked the pilots of the aircraft carrier USS *Bon Homme Richard.* They were a gutsy bunch who always gave us a good show. We received word that the carrier was available for a strike in our sector and our commanders picked Old Baldy as the target. My brother told me about this strike, and my driver, Nick O'Reilly, and I were there to watch at the appointed time. They really worked that hill over, and the Chinese were quick to go into their deep tunnels to safety. O'Reilly said, "Good God, look at that!" He pointed down our lines, and the hills were all topped by Americans watching the extended air strike. Just then, I glanced on down the Chinese lines to the other hills next to Old Baldy and I really could not believe my eyes. On every Chinese hill other than Old Baldy the Chinese soldiers were watching and gesturing just as the Americans were on their side of the line. What a strange war! I wondered why the air controllers did not switch targets to the other hills in a big hurry, but they did not. We could have gotten hundreds of them, bunched up on top of those hills like they were. Sometimes it seemed that we did everything the hard way over there.

Another time, an Australian P-51 Mustang was on a strafing mission in our sector. That plane was a propeller-driven fighter of World War II vintage, but still an effective airplane. The Aussie plane was hit by ground fire, and the pilot pulled up and bailed out into "no-man's

Foreboding Hill 200 or Pokkae Ridge is shown in the center of this photograph. Pokkae Ridge was fought over for months before it was finally captured by men of the 45th Infantry Division and made a part of the new advance outpost line of the American forces. It was during the battle for Pokkae Ridge in the spring of 1952 when Major General David L. Ruffner, the commander of the 45th, decided to strengthen the division's frontlines, that Frank L. Garrison, the cousin of the author, was severely wounded.

The treeless peak in the foreground is Hill 255, better known to the Thunderbirds as Old Baldy. The Americans lost many men fighting for Old Baldy, but the Chinese lost many more. Between June of 1952 and March of 1953 five battles were fought over Old Baldy. In the background is Hill 265, which was 10 meters higher in elevation than Old Baldy. That was what the soldiers faced in Korea. When they took a hill there always was a higher one right behind it.

Captain Harold Winburn using a Thunderbird "elevator" to climb an icy Korean hillside. Such contraptions were created to help in the fight against the Korean winter. Many a broken bone was caused by falls on icy mountainsides, and all sorts of clever ideas were put to use by the Thunderbirds.

Brigadier General Paul W. Reed, Jr., rose from the rank of private to general officer in the Thunderbird Division. He was a close friend of the author throughout his life. Reed was a lawyer and the Commissioner of Public Safety for the state of Oklahoma. His father, Paul W. Reed, Sr., held that position in earlier times.

land." Our infantry sent out a rescue patrol and brought the pilot back holding his opened parachute to his chest. When they reached our lines, the troops that had rescued the pilot asked him for a piece of his parachute as a souvenir. The Aussie solemnly replied, "Sorry old man, that's His Majesty's parachute." With that he asked for a ride back to division headquarters where he was picked up by his unit.

The Air Force had Forward Air Controllers who stayed with our ground units to advise and direct the pilots as to the targets involved. They had large radios mounted in their jeeps, and operated very much like our forward observers. Air and artillery kept us in the war. We fired artillery at even one enemy soldier if he showed himself. The Chinese never had that capability, either in the air or in artillery. They never learned how to mass fire the way we did it. For instance, we had a procedure called a Time on Target (TOT). When we found a particular inviting target involving a lot of troops in the open, we would locate it on our firing charts, which became very accurate and more so the longer we used them. We computed the time of flight of shells from each battery involved, and got all the batteries loaded and ready to shoot. The fire direction center gave each battery its time of flight, and started counting over the phone. When the time of each battery was reached, that battery would fire. Out on the receiving end, all the rounds of all the batteries firing reached the target at the same time. You can imagine what this did to the troops in the open, not being able to reach cover before they were hit by that tremendous firepower. That system was developed before World War II, and we really improved on it in Korea. Interestingly, the Germans and the Japanese had officers attending the Artillery School at Fort Sill who witnessed the first TOT ever shot, but neither army ever used the tactic. I am certainly glad they were not impressed, because that was an outstanding method of fire.

Only once did I have a chance to personally work over Chinese infantry in the open. I was up front with Giles Crisler, an officer in my battery, who previously had been in the Engineers. When he came to Korea, he was assigned as a forward observer in our battalion, the 171st. He had a very adept FO party, made up of Sergeant Donald J. Stacey, Private First Class Jerry T. McElroy, and Private First Class Harold G. Wills. Stacey was destined to be a teacher of history in the years to come, and McElroy had been a professional jockey and horse trainer from Colorado. They were close friends, even though their backgrounds were completely different. I am still in contact with both of them.

I went to the front to teach Giles the secrets of adjusting artillery fire. He proved to be an apt pupil. We worked our way around the enemy lines with 105-mm. shells, harassing and causing casualties. We had a battery commander's (BC) telescope up there in the observation post (OP) with us, and we could see the enemy lines very clearly. We had such overwhelming firepower that if there were any way at all to stay under cover, the Chinese troops would not show themselves.

Their trench system was awesome, and they were good at digging additions to it. We hardly ever saw any large numbers of the enemy for long periods of time.

But one particular day I zeroed the BC scope in on the top of a large hill in the enemy lines. There, circling the top of the peak, I saw maybe 20 shovels busily digging a trench. I could see the scoop of each shovel as dirt was thrown from the trench.

Second Lieutenant James R. Jack of Company B, 180th Infantry Regiment, sitting on the side of his jeep. At the wheel is Second Lieutenant William "Hook" Martin. Note the broom carried in the vehicle. The two lieutenants must have had the only clean jeep in Korea! Also note the mess kit on the hood of the jeep and the soldiers of Company B eating in the background. It obviously was "chow time."

Most every unit in the Thunderbird Division had a Korean orphan mascot. Battery B had "Cheesi" and Paul Reed of the Heavy Mortar Company of the 180th Infantry had this little boy, "Skoshie." Surprisingly, both of these names meant "little" in Japanese.

We called in a fire mission to the FDC, giving the coordinates of the target, as we figured them. The two ranging rounds fell 1,000 yards short of the target. Crisler and I were upset because we had misread our map. We added a thousand yards to the range, and the next two rounds hit right in the trench with that enemy work party. This was exciting, because we caught the enemy without overhead cover, where he tried never to be.

We called the whole battery into the shoot, and the next volley was from six guns instead of two. Again, the rounds landed in the middle of the diggers. We called "repeat fire for effect" several times, and the shells landed right where we wanted them. Finally, a very strange sight was presented to us. Those Chinese soldiers who were still ambulatory began jumping down the almost perpendicular sides of the hill. I could see their quilted caps with earflaps flapping as they hurtled 30 or 40 feet straight down. We screamed to the FDC for more fire, but they finally cut us off. We killed a lot of the enemy that day from the artillery fire or from the suicidal jump over the cliff. I will never forget that incident, and I do not think Crisler will either. We keep in contact with each other even today. Incidentally, he was an excellent soldier, and he was a brigadier general when he retired years later.

Unfortunately another target which we attempted to bring under fire that day shook our confidence a bit. Crisler, being an engineer, became interested in a large concrete dam which we could see plugging a gorge in the mountains over to the rear of the Chinese lines. Crisler located the dam on the very outer reaches of the battle maps we were issued. He computed that we could flood the Chinese units for miles around, if we could knock out that dam. I remembered that the 17th Field Artillery Battalion, armed with the very accurate and devastating eight-inch howitzer, had moved in down the valley from our battery. I calculated, correctly, that the big eight-inch howitzers could reach that dam. We decided that we would attack the dam and maybe drown a lot of the enemy.

We sent in a precision mission for the eight-inch howitzers, giving the coordinates of the big dam. The FDC gave us a "wait." We waited some time, and still no fire. I called back and asked what the delay was, and I was told that the target had to be cleared with Eighth Army. That was quite a thing to accomplish. In a few minutes, Eighth Army called back and said the target had to be cleared by United States Far East Theater Command (USFET). In other words, Tokyo! Finally the word came back, "mission denied." I was incredulous, and I asked, which was my right as an observer, "for what reason?" We then waited a long time, and finally we were told, "That target cannot be fired on, because destroying it would tend to disrupt the Korean economy." We were stunned, but there was nothing more we could do. We wondered, "What kind of a damn war is this? We cannot flood the enemy's lines, because it would disrupt the Korean economy. We were in North Korea. What the hell kind of a deal is this, anyway!"

Crisler was not the only general who came out of that mix. Another was my good and loyal friend of many years, Paul Reed, Jr. I attended the University of Oklahoma with Paul, where he was, among other things, the conference wrestling champion for two years. He was a delightful fellow, and was the Commissioner of Public Safety of Oklahoma and Commander of the Oklahoma Highway Patrol. He was a lawyer, as I am. Paul was in the 180th Infantry Regiment, and he was a natural leader.

Second Lieutenant James Jack, who grew up with Paul in Sulphur, Oklahoma, was in the same regiment. All of their lives, they were in friendly competition. The first combat patrol of the 180th was assigned to Second Lieutenant Jack. Paul volunteered to go on the next patrol, but the company commander squelched that saying, "We don't need two officers out there giving orders." Reed decided there was no way Jack was going to get ahead of him in this combat business. He took off his lieutenant's bars, and announced to all in attendance that he was going as a private rifleman! The company commander said, "Alright, but remember who is in charge."

The patrol left at dawn, snaking its way down the steep slope of Hill 334. The men got down into the valley, and were taken under heavy fire by the enemy. Reed was trapped in a very slight swale, and every time he showed himself in any way, small-arms fire zipped inches away from his head. For five long hours he was pinned down unable to move until American artillery suppressed the enemy fire, and Reed was able to join the rest of the patrol, which quickly executed "Howe Able," meaning in civilian terms H-A, which in doughfoot terms means "Haul Ass!"

The men in the patrol made it back to the main line of resistance completely bushed, and wiser all around. I asked Reed what he learned from that patrol and I will never forget his answer. "I'll never volunteer for another damn thing as long as I'm in Uncle Sam's Army." That was a lot of bunk, because he volunteered for a lot of things. Anyone who ever served either over or under Paul Reed knew him as a fine leader. I was proud to call him my friend.

CHAPTER 6

TOO MANY RATS

As soon as we arrived in Korea we became aware of a new disease which was proving to be 90 percent fatal to troops which contacted it. At least that was what we were told. It was called Hemorrhagic Fever by the Americans. It was a disease that caused the collapse of the capillaries all over the body of its victim. A person with the malady developed red blotches all over the body and became very weak and debilitated. The disease was first encountered by the Japanese Army when it was operating in China during World War II. They called it "Longo Fever," because they first encountered it along the Longo River in China. It was proving to be disastrous to our enemy, we were told, and it was rapidly becoming a very serious problem for us.

We anticipated that bubonic plague would be our burden in Korea, but that never developed for us. We were given a very painful immunization shot before we left Japan, and it seemed to be successful. I never knew of any American having the plague while I was in Korea. The intelligence reports told us that the enemy was having an epidemic of it just over across the lines. We sometimes heard enemy propaganda over the radio accusing us of spreading the plague among their troops, and they gave as a reason the fact that the soldiers of the 45th were given immunizing shots before coming to Korea. They even put a couple of very frightened GIs, whom they had captured when they overran our outpost out on Point Eerie, on the microphone to say that they had, indeed, had shots for the plague before they left Japan. This raised a big controversy internationally, but I assure you that we were not spreading disease of any kind among our enemy. They were pretty good at doing that for and to themselves.

Soon our medics learned how to treat Hemorrhagic Fever, and the death rate began to decrease. Before I came home we were told that the rate had been lowered to 10 percent among the troops that contacted it. We also learned that the disease was carried by the rats that infested the frontlines and the environs of the frontlines. The positions we took over from the First Cavalry Division had been occupied for a good while, and their area had become heavily rat-infested. There are not many good ways to stay clean up front, and it took a real

.Corporal Richard Bruneau, of Spokane, Washington, gives a "Hokkaido-style" haircut with hand-powered clippers to Sergeant First Class Alvin L. Latimer of McAlester, Oklahoma, while Battery B was still in Japan. The primitive living conditions on Hokkaido seemed like luxuries once the unit reached the frontlines in Korea.

On the left is Private First Class David N. Beckwermert and on the right is Corporal William T. Henderson, the clerks for Battery B. They are standing in front of the Quonset hut that served as the battery orderly room on Hokkaido. The Christmas tree on the right was never decorated because the battery was ordered to Korea before Christmas. The cold and snow in Japan was nothing compared to what the unit encountered on the frontlines in Korea.

First Lieutenant Denzil Garrison, on the left, and First Lieutenant Edgar J. Bradshaw standing in the snow in front of some Quonset huts on Hokkaido. Bradshaw was the executive officer of Battery B. Note the deep snow, which allowed the troops to train for the bitter cold of Korea. Although Hokkaido was not as luxurious as the southern islands of Japan, it was an excellent training ground for the war in Korea.

effort to keep a position free of the kind of refuse that attracts rats and other rodents. We re-dug all our dugouts, and abandoned the old First Cavalry Division "hootchies" as we called them. We started to get control of the rat problem after that.

Those rats were huge. They looked ever bit as large as cats, and we detested them. We burned all the old refuse piles left by our predecessors and we found huge nests of those damn rats at the bottom of every hole they had used to pile refuse and garbage. We learned that a gasoline fire would go a long way toward ridding us of those deadly pests. Although we griped at having to dig new shelters, we realized that it was certainly for our own well being. At least most of us felt that way about it.

There were all sorts of theories as to what caused the rats to be so huge. One accepted idea was that they were feeding on enemy corpses, which were strewn all over the hilltops after we had thrown the Chinese back. That was not the only reason, I am sure, but an awful lot of enemy corpses still laid around in inaccessible places, which probably have not all been found to this day. The Chinese and North Koreans were not nearly as considerate of their casualties, living and dead, as we were. At any rate, for whatever reason, the rats of Korea were huge and sometimes fearless.

I first encountered them when I awoke during my second week in Korea, and heard something up in a box I had placed up over my head in my dugout. I could hear something pulling candy bars from the box, which held my candy rations. I switched on a flashlight just in time to see a large rat pull a complete candy bar into a hole in the floor. Immediately we started to fill in every opening in the dugout we could find. We could never leave any edibles out in that dugout because those varmints would dig them out, one way or another. I was glad to move my bunk to the new hootchie when it was built. Once I was occupying that hoochie with Edgar Bradshaw, my battery executive officer. In the middle of the night I heard Bradshaw softly calling my name. He was zipped up in a heavy down sleeping bag, and his arms were not free. I switched on my flashlight, and there, perched on Brad's chest was a huge trench rat just looking him in the face. We were stunned. At least I was, and I am quite certain Bradshaw was, even more than I.

I had been awakened from a very sound sleep, and it took me a minute to get my senses together. I finally reached for my .45-caliber pistol, which was hanging in a shoulder holster over my bunk. Still sleepy I cocked the pistol and pointed it at that rat sitting on Bradshaw. The rat looked especially malevolent as he gazed into the light, twitching the long hairs on his snout.

Sleepy as I was, the pistol wavered a bit as I tried to aim at the rat. Bradshaw could see this in the feeble light, and decided that he did not want me shooting that rat off his chest. He whispered, "Throw your boot at it!" I reached under my bunk and grabbed my combat boot that I threw at the rat with all my might. The boot missed the rat completely and hit Bradshaw squarely in the head. The rat just sauntered out of the place almost contemptuously and went on about his business.

Bradshaw looked at me as he rubbed the knot on his head and said, "I'm damn glad you didn't shoot at him with your pistol." So was I, I assured him.

CHAPTER 7

THE COLDEST TASK

What I most remember about Korea was the cold. And the wind laden with ice, blowing out of Siberia at a tremendous speed. It seemed to go through everything before it. No matter how many layers of clothes we put on, we were always cold in the winter. If a person has never lived out in the open in temperatures many degrees below zero, it is difficult to imagine what it was like. To be caught without gloves, for instance, was a real danger. Anything you touched with bare hands in that kind of weather immediately froze to your hands. That can lead to tragic consequences.

One of the real problems we faced was the serving of the basic body functions. That is not much consequence when one lives in a comfortable home or building, but when living out in the open at minus 10 degrees, it becomes an item of vital significance. Just think, how does one go about using the toilet when out in the open, dressed in many layers of clothing, with the wind blowing ice in his face, and punishing any part of his body which is uncovered. That was a very serious problem. Believe me.

Our artillery ammunition was packed in wooden boxes made of sturdy yellow pine or spruce. When they were emptied, they made fine building material for the little privies that sprung up all over Korea. They were simply made. We either blasted or dug a hole about two feet in diameter, and built a little building over the top. Then we made a seat with a hole in the bottom. There were no doors on these struc-

A view of the main supply route leading from the frontlines in the area occupied by Battery B toward the rear area. This photograph was made in mid-winter and shows the snow and ice that covered the Korean mountainsides. Note the road on the left of the photograph that winds down the mountain to the valley toward the rear. The curving, icy roads became treacherous in the winter.

A typical "Korean War privy" was constructed from wooden shell crates that left cracks in the walls. However, because there was no door the cracks in the walls made little difference in the bitterly cold Korean winter. It was not uncommon for a soldier's buttocks to freeze to the seat. However, such contraptions were "better than nothing."

tures, and the wind would whip into them with a vengeance. The cracks between the ill-fitting boards allowed the inside to be just as cold, or colder, than the outside. When a GI went to relieve himself in one of those contraptions, sitting on ice-covered seats was brutal. We never figured how to get up off a freezing toilet without leaving a lot of skin stuck to the ice. We all had sore rears throughout the winter. We put off those absolutely necessary tasks as long as possible.

At first we had no urinals. Ammunition containers solved that problem, too. The shells, themselves, came packed in round metal canisters. We would knock the ends from them and bury them in the ground about a foot. Later we got fancy and covered the top with screen wire when we could find it. That way the insects were kept out of the tube. After a while, we set the tubes in gravel and that worked well. They certainly worked better than those abominable privies.

The infantry always came by to get wooden ammo boxes from us when we had any to spare. They were the preferred building materials of the UN Army. After a spirited firefight, we always had enough to furnish our infantry. But in quiet times the boxes were scarce. In the last week I spent with our battery, we got into the fight out on Pork Chop, and later Old Baldy. We fired 7,000 rounds in that week and the ammunition boxes were piled up "house-high" all around our battery. The infantry were there in numbers carting away those precious wooden boxes. I will bet to this very day there are Korean houses constructed from our ammunition boxes still standing.

Another thing we used secretly to keep warm was the unused powder charges from our ammunition. These made a bright and warm fire for a very short while, when one knew how to use them. Although such use was strictly prohibited, I am sure our cannoneers burned a lot of those things in the coldest part of winter. That was all right with me as long as they did not hurt themselves.

There is nothing in this world which can compare to the American GI as far as resourcefulness is concerned. He will make most any place a lot better given a little time. It was a privilege to be able to lead American soldiers. They are always just a little better than whoever and whatever is their foe. They will always find a way.

CHAPTER 8

OUR FAVORITE LEADER

Our battalion, the 171st, was assigned as the regular direct support artillery for the 180th Infantry Regiment. I had an inherited love for that regiment, because my father commanded the Second Battalion of the 180th Infantry during World War II. His heart was broken when he was taken away from the 45th Division and shipped overseas as a replacement officer, before the division went to war in the invasion of Sicily. I felt that I was a part of that Regimental Combat Team for a lot of reasons, including the service of my father. As Commander of Battery B my unit was in direct support of the Second Battalion, my father's old outfit. I took a lot of pride in that, and so did my father.

Many of the officers of the 180th had served under my father, and they were close to me for that reason. The Regimental Commander, Colonel James O. Smith, had been a first lieutenant and captain under my father in the early years of World War II. I felt a close relationship with him, and to this day I think he was the consummate infantry commander. He led a great team, and I was proud to be a small part of it. As a matter of fact, I still am.

J. O. Smith was a real physical specimen. We always believed that he could whip any man in his regiment, and so did those men who were fortunate enough to serve under him. He never had to prove that, of course, because he was loved and respected by all of us. Broad shouldered, lantern jawed, and muscled up on his frame, he looked squat from a distance, but he really was not. He was actually pretty tall, and truly a hell of a man. The epitome of an infantry combat leader. He was tough, plain spoken, and beating in his chest was a heart that loved those who served under him. He was a football player in his collegiate days, and he looked the part. In his regiment was his son, Sergeant Jerry D. Smith, who everyone liked and respected, because he asked for no special favors, which he probably would not have gotten if he had.

The 180th was the first regiment in the lines over in Korea, and on 11 December 1951, only four days after the regiment arrived, Sergeant Smith and another soldier, Frank C. Hudson, were cutting wood for fortifications, when Hudson stepped on a "bouncing betty" land mine. A bouncing betty was designed to fire into the air when triggered, and explode at about head height. Hudson was killed outright, and Jerry Smith was grievously wounded. He was evacuated to Japan, and still bears the scars of that mine detonation. A third soldier, Joseph L. Stegner, lost his leg in that explosion. Those were the first casualties of the 180th Infantry Regiment in Korea. Colonel Smith just helped evacuate his son, and hard as it must have been, went about his duties. That made us love him all the more.

Colonel Smith was one of those fellows who attracted nicknames. Among his were, "Uncle Shiloh," "Cotton," "Bulldog," and what he was called by his artillery, "Heavy J.O." That was a term of respect, because we saw him as strong and formidable like heavy artillery. He exuded confidence, and he never showed fear in any situation. He was just what an American infantry regimental commander should have been.

When I could get away from my battery, I called Colonel Smith through the regimental switchboard, to see if I could come up to visit him. We enjoyed our visits, and he always asked about my father. One particular visit sticks out in my mind. Colonel Smith had an open letter in his hand when I arrived. He showed me the letter he had received from a widow woman in upstate New York. It was 3 May 1952. The lady wrote about her only surviving son, Private Samuel P. Pizzo. She explained that he lost his only brother in World War II, and had joined in spite of this. She went on to say that he was not a physically strong boy, and she wanted to know if Colonel Smith could make him his driver and get him off the front for the rest of his time in Korea. The Colonel said he intended to do just that.

After reading the letter, Colonel Smith went up front to get Private Pizzo. He arrived at the Company E position, which was on "White Horse Mountain," another famous landmark of the Korean War. He asked the company commander if he could talk with young Pizzo. The CO told Colonel Smith that Pizzo was a replacement who had not been with the company long and was out on a patrol that was coming in even now. He pointed down to the forbidding terrain feature known as the "Alligator Jaws," below on the valley floor. The patrol snaked its way up the Jaws, single file, and staying under cover when it could. Just as the patrol was nearing the company position, one round of heavy mortar came in on top of them. That round struck one of the soldiers directly on his helmet, and Colonel Smith ran to the stricken soldier and carried him in.

One look told the colonel that the soldier was done, and he breathed his last breath in the colonel's arms. Colonel Smith looked at the company commander and asked, "Who was this man"? The company commander answered, "That was Private Pizzo, sir." Colonel Smith turned away from the soldiers there, and looked for a long time out over the battlefield. Finally, he wiped his eyes, and told the company commander to write his mother. As he told me of this melancholy occasion, he said one of the saddest things he would ever do was to answer the letter he held in his hand. I knew that he dreaded that job, but I also knew he would say the right things to that widow lady who had just lost her only surviving son.

When Colonel Smith received his well-earned orders to give up command of the regiment, and to prepare for shipment back home, we were all apprehensive as to what would happen to us when we lost our best and bravest warrior. In the 171st Field Artillery Battalion, we hated to lose him just as much as his men in the 180th Infantry did. When the appointed day arrived, we placed a lookout down the road to let us know when Colonel Smith's jeep came into sight. We had already set up a most impressive goodbye for him. We asked the FDC

Colonel James O. Smith of Okemah, Oklahoma, commanded the 180th Infantry Regiment. One of the first three casualties of the regiment was his son, Jerry Smith, who was seriously wounded by a mine that killed one soldier and blew the leg off of another. Colonel Smith was everything a combat commander should be. His men always came first with him and they loved him for it. Battery B was a part of the 180th Regimental Combat Team.

After sailing through the Panama Canal and across the Pacific, the 45th Division was stationed at Chitose, Hokkaido, Japan. Battery B was a part of the division that was teamed with the 180th Infantry to form the 180th Regimental Combat Team. This photograph was taken in front of the headquarters of the Second Battalion, 180th Infantry Regiment at Chitose. On the left is Lieutenant Colonel Ellis B. Richie, of Norman, Oklahoma, who later became commander of the 180th Infantry Regiment. He was an excellent leader and soldier. On the right is Captain Russel P. Lipe of Okemah, Oklahoma.

to pick out a good target for us to shoot at, and we laid all six guns of the battery on that suspected gathering point over in the enemy sector.

As Colonel Smith passed down the road in front of the battery, I stepped out and saluted him, and at the same time our battery executive officer, Edgar J. Bradshaw, ordered the guns to begin firing, one at a time, from right to left, at five second intervals. When each gun had fired three times, Bradshaw called "cease fire," and all of the cannoneers came to attention and saluted. Colonel Smith was pleased, to say the least, and he returned our salutes with a wry smile on his face. He had just been given an 18-gun salute with live ammunition. I do not know of that ever being done before or after. I have often wondered what the Chinese must have thought, when all at once 18 rounds of 105-mm. projectiles came ripping at them, and at five second intervals. They probably thought we were crazy, and we probably were.

CHAPTER 9

THE ARTILLERY WAR

At times we were so close to the enemy that the infantry used to say they could smell them. Usually, though, we were hundreds of yards away from enemy lines, reaching our adversaries only with our air and artillery. I have heard many an infantryman say that they loved the artillery, because it was always there in rain, snow, sleet, or what have you. They loved it when we gave them support at times when it was too dark or dreary for the Air Force to be up. I do not exaggerate when I say that the artillery was the deciding arm in the Korean War. Without it we would have been driven off the peninsula. Most any Korean veteran will tell you that.

Our forward observers were right up there with them. In a minute they could have accurate, deadly fire laid where it was needed. We were a part of what the Army called the same combat team—the 180th Infantry and the 171st Field Artillery.

When the war wound down to a static situation, we really played into the Chinese hands. They were in a desperate situation when they finally said they wanted to go to the "peace table," and the so-called "truce" was not a truce at all. It was an unearned chance on the part of the enemy to build his army back up, and to replenish his supplies.

It is sobering to contemplate that we lost more men after we went to the peace table than we lost before we went there. Constant attrition and casualties add up, and we lost men who might have been saved, if we had gone on and finished the enemy off after we started pushing the Chinese back toward the north. But we did not, probably because of political considerations as much as anything else. I hope we never make the same mistake again.

The Chinese Army that we fought had the advantage of always having more men than we had. Their system of logistics and supply was, however, archaic and primitive. We found that out when the Chinese went on an offensive, they worked for weeks bringing shells and other weapons up laboriously by hand. Each replacement coming to the front carried one or two artillery shells on his back, and in this way they could slowly stockpile a supply. They would hit hard that first day, and usually they were successful in breaching our outer defenses. We, by plan, had an alternate line established about a mile behind the first, and our plan was to withdraw to those new positions if the pressure got too heavy. Then, there was a third line established behind the second, which would be utilized if needed. That line was to be held at all costs.

The Chinese soldier carried five days of food and ammunition rations with him when he attacked. We learned this, and we contained them one way or another for five days. After that, they were almost at our mercy. Our superior logistics, especially in ammunition and food, made quick work of those poor devils when they reached "the end of their string." General Ridgway adopted this approach after he took command in Korea. We could not lose that way, but we also were denied victory. A stalemate is a trying thing for an American soldier to endure.

When General Ridgway took over after General MacArthur was replaced, a new approach was tried. The losses of our troops were disastrous to the Truman administration in those days, and they responded by stopping our troops in their tracks in order to hold down on casualties. So the UN command began a slow and deliberate drive to retake Seoul, which it did, and to liberate almost all of South Korea, which it also did. A very small bit of South Korea was left in Communist hands, and quite a slice of North Korea was left in UN control. This was calculated to allow the Chinese and North Koreans to save face, which was and is all-important to the Oriental psyche. By

First Lieutenant Blair E. Rollin of Norristown, Pennsylvania, was a replacement officer who came to Battery B shortly after the unit arrived in Korea. Rollin was a forward observer and later battery executive officer. He was a very popular officer with both the men and fellow officers. The author searched for Rollin for years after Battery B returned from Korea, before he was finally located back in Pennsylvania from whence he came.

leaving a corner of South Korea in their hands, the UN commander allowed the North to claim a stalemate. On our side, the line across Korea where the offensive ended was much more defensible than the original boundary on the 38th parallel.

Our leaders knew we could never match the Chinese and North Koreans in numbers. What we could match them in, and did match them in, was firepower. Our artillery was superior to theirs, and we knew so much more about sophisticated fire direction than they did. Their firing techniques were primitive, and they never learned to mass their fires the way our artillery units did. We even surveyed in our infantry's 4.2-inch mortars and blended them into our fire control operations.

The 4.2-inch mortar was originally developed as a chemical mortar in World War II, and it was found to be a very accurate weapon. As a matter of fact, it was the most effective mortar in our arsenal. It was a rifled weapon, where the other mortars were smoothbore. This made the 4.2 much more accurate than other more conventional mortars, and they could be just as accurate as our light artillery. Our Regimental Mortar Company became an integral part of our artillery fire plan.

One of the limitations of the 4.2-inch mortar was that its range, though longer than other mortars, was still quite a lot shorter than the 105-mm. howitzer, which was our basic light artillery weapon. Still, for close-in support to be dropped in the valleys at the base of our mountaintop front-line, it was a great weapon. Another limitation was that the 4.2-inch could not fire ammunition with the variable-time (VT) fuse, which had been used to such a devastating effect in the latter battles of World War II.

The VT-fuse was a marvel. Each shell transmitted a radio beam before it in its flight, and when the shell came within 20 yards of the ground, it automatically detonated. These airbursts, as they were known, were devastating to troops in the open. Just about any mass attack by the Chinese could be broken up with VT-fused ammunition. This changed the entire complexion of the ground war in Korea. We had plenty of artillery, and we would expend whatever ammunition necessary to hold down on our casualties and inflict the maximum loss on the enemy.

The infantry loved that fuse, even if a pretty high proportion of those radio shells went off somewhere down the gun-target line, short of the target. When the weather was cloudy, that happened fairly often. Still, the VT-fuse was an awesome weapon. I have often wondered if such a fuse has been developed for heavy mortars by now. Maybe they have such advanced weapons now that such would not be practical. But in Korea, the Chinese prisoners would tell us that Americans had "automatic artillery," just as the German infantry described it in World War II. Our artillery with its advanced fire direction techniques and the VT-fuse kept us in the fight against the overwhelming numbers of Chinese soldiers we faced. We took pride in that, and our infantry knew our value, and appreciated us for it.

Another innovation we used was the coordination of the fires of the quad .50-caliber machine guns used by the 145th Anti-Aircraft Battalion. The quad .50 was a fearsome weapon that mounted four .50-caliber machine guns on an armored half-track chassis. The .50-caliber was the heaviest machine gun in our arsenal, and it kicked out a heavy and death-dealing slug that would penetrate anything but heavy armor. It was disastrous to light vehicles and troops in the open. Its four machine guns were mounted two on top and two about 18 inches blow the top. When fired on full automatic, the slugs would decimate an area as big as a city block.

We surveyed these weapons in, and adjusted them in on suspected targets. We entered the quad .50s on our fire control charts, and began to use them to interdict crossroads, suspected headquarters areas, and other such targets. They were devastating to the Chinese. Once, our Chinese interpreter heard them begging on the radio, "Turn off the Running Water." This was their call sign for quad .50 fire. We stopped a Chinese attack cold that night, with those quad .50 concentrations.

The 145th adopted "Running Water" as the motto on their battalion crest. Because we had no need for protection from Chinese or North Korean air attack we were happy to put those fearsome fifties to work against ground troops. This we did, and most effectively.

Then, of course, we had complete control of the air. Our Air Force, that was made a separate branch of service after World War II, came through with flying colors. The naval aviators were especially effective in ground troop support, and we loved their strikes that came in from aircraft carriers steaming in the waters off Korea. It was fascinating to watch the actions of the pilots as they came in to strafe the enemy lines that were heavily defended by anti-aircraft guns. Some would practically fly down into the trenches while others would strafe from a much safer altitude. We used to say about the "brave" ones, "There's a bachelor who doesn't give a damn!" And when one of the less daring made his strafing run, we would say, "There's a guy with a wife and four kids, who is eligible to go home next week!" At any rate, we were happy to have them all on our side.

The three Forward Observer Sections of Battery B on Hokkaido. Front row, left to right: Private First Class Orlind S. Case, Sergeant Donald J. Stacey, Sergeant Jesse C. McGee, Private First Class Jerry T. McElroy. Second row, left to right: First Lieutenant James M. Crabtree, Second Lieutenant George Chesnut, and Second Lieutenant William R. Sumter. When Battery B took over its position on the frontlines in Korea, the forward observers were assigned to infantry units so that they could call in artillery fire for support.

General Matthew B. Ridgway became the Commander of the Eighth Army after the death of Lieutenant General Walton W. Walker, who was a tanker and had served under Lieutenant General George S. Patton in World War II. Lieutenant General Walker was killed in a motor vehicle accident on 23 December 1950. His replacement was General Matthew Ridgway, who was replaced by General James A. Van Fleet after MacArthur was removed from command. Ridgway replaced MacArthur.

Captain James A. Van Fleet, Jr. served as a pilot in a squadron of what we knew as A-26 light bombers. Later, they became known as the B-26, and were a mainstay in our aerial arsenal. But on a cold and clear night in April of 1952, I heard a flight of A-26 planes fly over our battery on into North Korea. That night, Captain Van Fleet's plane disappeared and nothing was ever heard from the crew. I have always believed that I heard the flight of Captain Van Fleet as he flew to his destruction that night. I had an opportunity to tell his father about what happened that night in a telephone conversation I had with him years later. General Van Fleet was still very aggrieved by the loss of his son, and he seemed to appreciate that I still remembered. He was a fine leader, who would have won a complete victory over the Communists in the field, if he had been left to his own capabilities without political interference.

I have nothing but praise for him as Eighth Army Commander. General Van Fleet became disgusted with political interference in the conduct of the war, and coupled with the loss of his son he had ample reason to retire, in February of 1953. Upon retirement, he said that he could have won the war in 1951, if he had been given backing by the politicians. Having been there at that time, I believed him.

CHAPTER 10

THE REGULARS TAKE OVER

Point Eerie was well named. It was a little "pimple" on the end of a most imposing landmass rising above the Korean river plain. It stuck out like a sore thumb way out in enemy country, rising some 50 or 60 feet above the rest of the end of T-bone Mountain. It was not easily occupied by either the Chinese or us. Once you were set up on Eerie, you were right in the middle of a bulls-eye unable to be reinforced or supported except by artillery. It was a lonely place that we patrolled around for several months after we took over the front from the First Cavalry Division.

In early 1951 the decision was made to occupy Eerie permanently. A platoon of the 179th Infantry Regiment fortified it. They had occupied it several weeks when the Chinese attacked with a reinforced company. The Chinese were able to get into the position because the Thunderbirds mistook the movement of enemy troops as a patrol which was to pass that way at approximately the same time. The platoon was overrun, and captured almost to a man. When a relief force took over Eerie the next morning, only a few survivors were found. In the dust was found the second lieutenant bars of the platoon commander, where he had thrown them to mislead the enemy captors as to his identity.

This action worried the entire division. We realized that we were facing a determined enemy, skillful in tactics, and developing into a stronger foe daily. Every replacement they brought in had two rounds of 76-mm. ammunition on his back, and slowly they built up their ammunition supply until they could lay down a heavy barrage, in their style. They fired flat trajectory artillery at point blank range. Although they could not mass their fires like we did, they could still cause casualties by means of their single pieces, sighting on our strong points. We learned a lot from the loss of that platoon and it never happened that way again.

When our division commander, Major General James C. Styron, was rotated home, we were assigned a new commander, Major General David L. Ruffner, a Regular Army officer. I was told that he looked at the battle map back in division headquarters and pushed his open hands out into enemy country and said something like, "We'll push out here to strengthen our line." His outstretched hands covered the biggest part of an entire Chinese Field Army, and we knew we were in for trouble. Our casualties increased the day Major General Ruffner took command. He made a fateful decision that our first move would be to permanently occupy Hill 255, known as Old Baldy.

For some time we would occupy that hill in the daytime, and the Chinese would occupy it at night. Each side was rather careful to be punctual in coming and leaving, so as not to cause casualties. Major General Ruffner had other ideas. He ordered the 180th Infantry Regiment to stay out on Old Baldy for good when they next went out there. That was just what they did, although everybody knew we were starting a fight.

Company B, 180th Infantry Regiment, was sent out to permanently occupy the hill. By this time I had been moved from my Battery B into the battalion FDC, where I was assigned as the assistant S-3 fire control officer for the battalion. The way we broke down the assignment was that I was in charge of the fire direction center at night, and the S-3 was in charge during the day. This proved to be a fateful plan for me.

When the Chinese came in to occupy the hill at nightfall, they were met by heavy fire and resistance from the men of Company B. The Chinese platoon was cut to ribbons, and driven away from Baldy with very heavy casualties. We dumped hundreds of rounds of artillery

Seated in the jeep on the left is First Lieutenant Denzil Garrison. On the right is Battery B's First Sergeant and Garrison's valued friend, John T. Dunn, of McAlester, Oklahoma. Garrison readily admitted that whatever success Battery B achieved was largely due to the leadership and hard work of First Sergeant Dunn. This photograph was taken while the battery was training on Hokkaido. In the background is a 105-mm. howitzer hooked to a two and a half ton truck. Members of Battery B are preparing a firing position for the howitzer.

around the perimeter and created a "ring of steel" which took the Chinese unit by complete surprise.

The Chinese did not take to our plan very well. On the second night, a reinforced infantry company of Chinese hit Old Baldy with a vengeance. Again, we dumped hundreds of rounds of VT-fused shells into the midst of the attackers, and Company B held the hill. We knew that the enemy would be back because he did not mind losing troops as much as we did and the thing the Chinese had the most of was men. By this time I was pretty worn out. We fired all night for two nights, and we were bushed. Still we thought we knew what lay ahead of us on the third night. We were not wrong in our assessment.

The third night, the Chinese again attacked. This time a reinforced battalion hit beleaguered B Company with the full weight of over a thousand screaming Chinese blowing bugles and sending colored flares into the air. That was the way they communicated for the most part, having few radios in their units. This was cumbersome, but no one who has heard a Chinese bugle blowing in the Korean night will ever forget the mournful sound that seemed to penetrate into one's innards. It was a psychological weapon that left its mark on the Americans that they never forgot.

From pure numbers, the Chinese were able to overrun the command post bunker of Company B. Our forward observer was in that bunker, and he was calling in fire by means of a field telephone. As often happened, the field telephone wire was soon cut, either by artillery, mortars, or by enemy wire cutters who were assigned that duty. When that wire went out, the observer called in by radio, and we kept up the heavy VT-fire around the bunker.

Abruptly, about three in the morning, the voice of the observer could not be heard any more. The base radio set in the fire direction center became quiet. There was a red light, however, on that set which burned when a transmission was being sent or received. We could see the blinking red light on the front of the set, spelling out "SOS," time after time. Our observer was in trouble. We realized that the enemy had overrun the command bunker, and that the Chinese were on top of the position. That meant that they had no overhead cover and were

The command post of Company G, 180th Infantry Regiment, in the lower right, as seen from Hill 233, where Battery B maintained an observation post. Note that the roads are easily seen behind the American lines, together with vehicles and fortifications. The Chinese did not have this luxury because of American artillery and air supremacy.

in the open. Our men, we hoped, were in the bunkers, safer from our fire than were the attackers.

I was the sole officer in the fire direction center, and I made the decision to fire on the CP directly with VT-fuse, which we did. Volley after volley were sent directly atop the bunkers with us praying that none of our men would be hurt due to the overhead cover they had.

My battalion commander, who was known as the "Old Maid" by the troops, came excitedly into the FDC, exclaiming, "What are you shooting at?" He looked at the map, and shouted, "My God, you're shooting directly on B Company!" I explained what had happened, and why we were shooting on the position of our infantry. He was very excited and exclaimed that I had better be right. I told him that he could order the fire stopped if he wished, but I did not recommend it. He chewed on his cigar and said that because we had already started the fire, he would not stop it, and the error had already been made before he came in. I knew that if everything went to pieces, I was in for trouble. To tell the truth, I did not trust the "Old Maid" to back me up to any extent, if things did not turn out right. The S-3 came into the bunker and told the "Old Maid" that my decision was correct.

In a few minutes, the radio came alive, and our observer excitedly reported that the VT had cut the enemy to pieces. He reported 63 enemy dead atop the command bunker, and the enemy in full retreat from the hill. The door to the sandbagged FDC burst open, and

Colonel Ellis B. Richie, the 180th Infantry Regimental commander, strode in. He said, "Colonel, that VT out on Hill 255 saved B Company tonight." The "Old Maid" took his well-chewed cigar out of his mouth and said, "It was a hell of a chance to take, but I knew we had to take it." I was speechless. I threw open the door and stood outside gulping the cold night air. It was not an easy thing to do, firing on my own comrades. Finally, I let go, and the tears flowed down my cheeks. Every one of the men in that fire direction center, including Colonel Richie, knew that the battalion commander was taking credit for something he doubted and wanted to stop. Dawn came, mercifully, and the night crew sunk into deep sleep, completely worn out.

CHAPTER 11

THE PIPER LAURIE CAPER

A tour in Korea was a long time for a young GI to go without seeing an American woman. Realizing this, Special Services brought movie stars over from time to time. Usually, the front-line soldiers did not get to see them, but they came and put on shows for the division rear and later for the rest camps. I remember clearly the only one I ever saw. In the summer of 1952, word came to our airstrip situated near the division headquarters that the beautiful young starlet, Piper Laurie, was to fly in by light plane around noon on a day certain in about a week. My friend, Bill Sumter, let me know the good news, and I saw fit to be visiting back at the airstrip for the noon meal on the fateful day.

We all talked about what we would say if we got to actually meet Piper, and she was the main topic of conversation for at least three days before she arrived. I was not the only one who found a reason to be around the airstrip at the

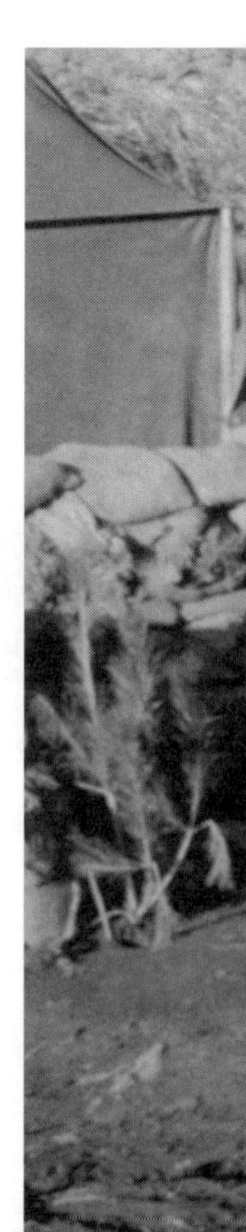

A tour in Korea was a long time for a young GI away from home. Christmas of 1951 was a bleak time for many Thunderbirds; however, in an attempt to maintain some holiday spirit a Christmas tree was put up and decorated with homemade items fashioned from cards received from home. Note the sandbags around the tent to provide protection from enemy shellfire. In the upper right of the photograph, behind the tent, is a privy.

appointed time. The mess tent was crowded with a lot of anxious young guys, each dreaming of getting a chance to meet a real live starlet from "Uncle Sugar" as we called the United States.

I went through the chow line there in the mess tent where meals were served and filled the large metal tray I was given with all sorts of good Army chow, including a T-bone steak, which was also a special treat to me. I had just sat down at the long mess table, when a beautiful Piper Laurie came in the tent, hauntingly attractive to us, even in the ill-fitting Army fatigues she wore. We were all speechless, and we wondered where she was going to sit.

Unbelievably, she marched right down to my table and sat next to me. I was ecstatic. My hands trembled and the perfume she wore almost caused me to swoon. I reached to move my tray of food, including my precious T-bone, and of all things I turned it over in my lap. Everyone there, including gorgeous Piper Laurie, died laughing. I

An infantry battalion command post under construction in Korea. The double thick sandbag walls provided protection from everything but a direct hit from artillery and a degree of warmth during the Korean winter. The soldier on the right is hauling filled sandbags from a pile and putting them on top of the bunker's wall while the other two soldiers are using the bags to build the walls higher.

excused myself, and left the chow tent accompanied by the guffaws of my comrades. I would like to ask her if she remembers that occasion, because I have and always will.

Although it seemed rather a waste to some for those USO people to come over there to see us in that God-forsaken place, it was most appreciated by the troops, even by the front-line troops who did not get the chance to see them. They really did help to restore the nerves of those troops who made it back to rest camps, and the entertainers seemed to enjoy seeing us, even though they had to perform in some very awkward places.

CHAPTER 12

A TANK WAS SUNK

The division airstrip was a popular place with me. I had several good friends there, and I liked to visit them. Along with Bill Sumter, there was Gene Short, another first lieutenant from my battalion, who had been in the Army Air Corps in World War II. He was older than Bill, having served overseas for 48 months in that war. By the time he was sent home, he had an astounding total of 56 months overseas, in combat zones. For a "citizen soldier," that was about the maximum any of us, including Gene Short, had ever heard of. Being an old "fly boy," Gene was a natural to become a valuable and first class artillery air observer.

The job of an artillery air observer was to fly over our lines, watching the enemy's front, and adjust artillery fire on any targets that presented themselves to the watchful eyes of the observer. It was a bit dangerous, but very exciting work. And it had the added advantage of furnishing a comfortable cot to sleep in, and the chow was excellent. They all seemed to be satisfied with their assignment. As a qualified artillery observer, I looked forward to the several opportunities I had to fly missions with our air section from time to time. I almost did that once too often. But more about that later.

One icy cold winter day, Gene Short was flying near T-bone Mountain. He spotted a gun emplacement at the very top of one of the peaks of T-bone. He called in a fire mission, requesting fire from the 189th Field Artillery Battalion, which was our medium artillery bat-

A disabled enemy tank in no man's land in Korea. The tank first was disabled by an anti-tank mine and then destroyed by artillery fire. The most useful weapon against enemy armor was artillery fire and within a few months of the outbreak of fighting in Korea many communist tanks had been destroyed and the survivors were kept well hidden from artillery observers.

A disabled American M4 Sherman medium tank in no man's land. The tank was disabled by an enemy anti-tank mine. Fortunately the crew survived. The 35-ton Sherman, which had been introduced in World War II, was the main American battle tank during the Korean War. It was armed with a 76-mm. main gun, a 50-caliber M2 heavy machine gun on top of the turret, and a .30-caliber medium machine gun in the hull.

talion utilizing the 155-mm. howitzer, as distinguished from the 105-mm. howitzers that were fired by our three light artillery battalions. The larger shells of the 155-mm. howitzers were more effective against fortifications and armor than were the 105-mm. howitzers, which were very effective against troops in the open. Many a mass "suicide attack" of the Chinese and North Koreans were stopped cold by the light 105-mm. howitzers. However, this particular target seemed to call for the heavier 155-mm. shells

As Gene adjusted the fire in on the gun emplacement, several of his rounds sailed over the top of the peak and into the valley behind T-bone. What he did not know was that the enemy had established a tank park in that protected area and those rounds that went over the top landed in the middle of that tank park. The Chinese tankers thought they had been discovered, and the tanks scattered in all directions like huge cockroaches. Gene was astounded to see this, and he immediately took them under fire from the 155-mm. howitzers.

Most of the tanks scurried behind the next hill, but one of them foolishly drove out on the ice of the frozen river that ran through our sector. Gene "zeroed" in on this tank, and landed a round right behind it. Then he landed the next round right in front of it. The Chinese driver was stopped. He could not go forward, because there was a huge hole in the ice caused by the terrific penetration of the 155-mm. shell. He could not back up, because there was another large hole in the ice behind him. Gene then ordered "fire for effect" straddling the tank and knocking more holes in the ice. Finally, the ice under the tank gave way, and the tank sunk to the bottom of the deep river. Gene recalled the famous words of the Navy pilot in World War II, after he had sunk a German submarine—"Sighted sub, sank same." He paraphrased that famous report by calling in to the fire direction center the laconic account, "sighted tank, sank same." This made the division newspaper.

A 155-mm. howitzer crew of the 189th Field Artillery Battalion. The 155-mm. howitzer was used in general support and to inflict heavy punishment on the enemy throughout World War II, Korea, and Vietnam. It had a sustained rate of fire of 40 rounds per hour with a maximum range of more than 7 miles and is still used, in one form or another, today. It was a 155-mm. howitzer of the 189th Field Artillery Battalion that was used to sink a Chinese tank as it crossed a frozen river in Korea in the Battery B area of the frontlines.

CHAPTER 13

AN UNLUCKY ALLY

There were soldiers from many nations fighting with us against the communists in Korea. Filipinos, French, English, Canadian, Thai, Belgian and Turkish soldiers were all there in the UN Army. This led to some communication difficulty and some supply problems, but overall it turned out pretty well.

Each of the Allied Armies had its own peculiarities, strengths, and weaknesses. For example, the French unit was only in battalion size, but those soldiers were the pick of the French Army. They were superb soldiers, but there were very few of them. The Filipinos were picked men, also. They would come in, serve six months, and be replaced by other Filipinos. They fought to serve, because such service provided them with American veteran status, including hospitalization and retirement if they were wounded. The Filipino artillery battalion that was attached to us was a good one. They used American weapons and American firing techniques.

The Thai unit was an interesting group. They hated the cold weather more than the others did. This led to a memorable experience for one of our forward observers. He was assigned to go out on a far-reaching patrol with the Thai battalion, as their artillery observer. They went a long way out in no-man's land, and the Thais became cold. They just stopped and built a fire right out in front of the enemy. Our observer called in and asked what he should do, and he was told to get back to our lines post haste. We fired a protective barrage, and the patrol came on in, unscathed, and probably warm.

Enigmatic faces of the Korean Service Corps (KSC) soldiers, who were assigned to units of the 45th Infantry Division as laborers. They were hardy, sometimes almost sullen, but useful. They carried ammunition and equipment up the Korean mountainsides on simple A-frames strapped to their backs. They often carried more than their own weight. KSC troops certainly made the lot of the American soldier much easier. Their quilted uniforms and caps provided protection from the frigid Korean winter weather.

The ruins of Seoul, the capital of South Korea. Seoul was overrun by communist forces and liberated by UN troops three times between the summer of 1950 and the summer of 1951. The bitter fighting left much of the city nothing but rubble.

The English and Canadian soldiers gave a good account of themselves. Their artillery was good, and their infantry worked well with us. Their fight on the Imjin River in 1951 was a classic. Their losses were high, and the enemy learned about British firepower in that action. They were professional soldiers, and their actions showed it.

Perhaps the hardiest soldiers of them all were the Turks. They were feared by the North Koreans and the Chinese, and they always gave a good account of themselves. They seemed to know no fear, and they had no command for retreat. To get them to withdraw, the Turks were pointed in the desired direction and told to advance. They were trained never to retreat under any circumstance. Their system of court-martial was simple. They obeyed or they were shot.

A close friend of mine was an officer in the Quartermaster Corps. He ran a shoe repair depot about 60 miles behind the front. One morning, a Turkish soldier appeared at the depot, asking for food. My friend saw that he was a Turk, and ordered him to be fed at once. After awhile, he started to wonder what he was doing so far behind the front. Division headquarters was called, and a report on the Turk was made. In a short while, division called back and told my friend to get his name, which they passed on to the Turkish headquarters. In a short time, another call ordered the Turkish soldier placed under guard to await a detachment from the Turkish Army which was coming to get him.

In a few hours, a Turkish three-quarter ton truck showed up, with six armed infantrymen in the back. The sergeant in charge saluted my friend and took charge of the prisoner, which he identified as a deserter. The prisoner was then marched out into the open field next to the depot, and the sergeant ordered the six soldiers to form a firing squad. The miscreant was shot dead right there in front of the quartermaster shoe repairmen. The Turks then loaded up the body of the deserter and headed back to their unit. My friend swore he would never turn another Turk in, under any circumstance. I assure you that there were precious few deserters from the Turkish Army in Korea.

CHAPTER 14

RAILROAD TRACKS

In the summer of 1951 my morale began to flag. I had been commanding the battery as a first lieutenant for a long time, and I thought it was past time for me to be promoted. To tell the truth, I was feeling a bit sorry for myself.

We had been ordered to move from our original position to another sector of our front in order to keep in firing position in direct support of our regiment, the 180th, which had been moved to the left flank of the division. On the day of our move, we were given orders to leave an officer in charge of our old position to make certain it was left in proper order. I assigned Second Lieutenant Bob Baggett to the task. Shortly thereafter, we received word that Bob's father died back in the States. He was given an emergency leave and departed immediately. Not having another officer in the battery area, I assigned First Sergeant John Dunn to carry out the task of checking our old position as we left. I was sure he would do at least as good a job as any officer in the battery.

Our colonel, still known as the "Old Maid," sent the battalion executive officer, a major, to check our position. Seeing a first sergeant and not an officer, in charge, he sent for me. "Why wasn't an officer in charge at the old position?" I explained that Second Lieutenant Baggett had left that job on emergency leave, and I had no other officers available in the battery area. The major said, "That's a lie!" I became infuriated at this and told the major that he could go to hell as far as I was concerned. He got in his jeep and left.

Brigadier General Hal L. Muldrow, Jr., was the commander of the 45th Division Artillery in Korea. Muldrow, who later was promoted to Major General, was a Choctaw Indian and a true warrior. In his college days he was the captain of the University of Oklahoma football team. During World War II he commanded the 189th Field Artillery Battalion in Europe. He was highly decorated.

I knew I had made a monstrous error, and I awaited the consequences with much foreboding. Sure enough, I got a call on my radio to report to Parasol Six, the code name for Brigadier General Hal L. Muldrow, Jr. the division artillery commander. I knew I was in for at least a good ass chewing or perhaps a lot more. On the way to division artillery headquarters I took out my notebook and began to write down all the negative things I knew about the major, and I made what seemed a pretty impressive list. I decided that if I were going down, I would not be alone.

Brigadier General Muldrow was a second father to me. He was from my hometown of Norman, Oklahoma, and I had been his aide de camp until we were called to active duty. Then I was transferred to a firing battery because I was a two-time graduate of the Field Artillery School at Fort Sill. The general and I were fraternity brothers from the University of Oklahoma, and we were genuine friends.

I went to the headquarters tent and asked for the general. I was told that he was awaiting me in his command tent and that I should go

On the left is Corporal David N. Beckwermert of Patterson, New Jersey. He became a successful executive of an electric utility corporation after Korea. Seated with him is Second Lieutenant Claron H. Coleman, who received a battlefield commission in Korea. Coleman was the only member of Battery B to receive such a commission while the author was with the unit. Coleman is seated on an empty Coca Cola case and empty Coca Cola bottle is on the ground by Beckwermert. Coca Cola was made available whenever possible to help maintain morale.

there. I took out my notebook and looked it over on the way. I would let him know about that major, for sure.

I entered the tent, and Brigadier General Muldrow was sitting at a field table in the center of it. I saluted him and started to pull up a chair to sit in. The general said, "Who told you to sit down?" I jumped up at attention and awaited what I knew was coming. "What's this about you telling the major to go to hell?" I stammered, and took up my notebook to list all the awful things I remembered about the major. The general said, "Who told you to talk?" I stammered that no one had, and he said, "All right, be quiet then." By this time, I wanted nothing more than to get out of the tent and be on my way. "Do you have anything more to say?" I stammered that I had nothing more to add, and saluted and walked lamely toward the door.

The general said, "And another thing, you are out of uniform." I stopped and said I did not understand what was wrong with my uniform. He said, "You are wearing the wrong insignia." I just stood at attention, and hoped for the end to all this. The general walked over to me and said, "You are not even wearing the right bars." He reached up and roughly took off my first lieutenant bars and told me to leave. I stumbled to the door, longing to be outside. He said, "Wait a minute, you are going to have to have some insignia on your collar when you leave here." He walked over to me and pinned a new set of captain's bars on me. I was stunned, and relieved. I broke into a smile, and saluted the general again. He told me it was time for me to get back to my outfit, and I did an about face and turned to leave. The general said, "Captain, it isn't a very good idea for you to tell a major to go to hell." I mumbled that I would never do it again.

As I left the tent, there was the whole division artillery staff lined up with grins on their faces. I realized that I had been the butt of one of the great jokes of all time. Even the major had been in on it. I had played right into their hands. My temper, exacerbated by my self-pity, had made a fool of me. When I got back to the outfit, the men, and the major, were waiting to congratulate me. I mumbled a quick apology to him, which he graciously accepted. I had learned one of the great lessons of my life.

CHAPTER 15

ASLEEP AT THE WHEEL

Once I came very close to being captured. My driver, Nick O'Reilly, was sure of himself, in certain ways. As a matter of fact, he was "fearless" at times. We headed up to the headquarters of the 180th Infantry to see Colonel J.O. Smith, the regimental commander. We stayed tired most of the time, and being experienced soldiers we would go to sleep any time the occasion to do so presented itself. As the old saying goes, "An old soldier never walks when he can stand still, or stands when he could sit, or sits when he could lie down, or lies awake when he could be sleeping." The theory is that you had better get whatever rest you can, because you may not have another chance for a long time.

With that axiom in mind, I learned to sleep in a jeep as it made its way down the rocky and dusty roads of Korea. I am sure my men had a good nickname for me, and I have been told I was known as "The Sleeping Jesus," behind my back, of course.

This particular day, in the early afternoon, we were driving along the road, and I suddenly awakened with a start. I looked around, and did not recognize any familiar landmarks. I immediately felt uneasy and said to my driver, "Nick do you know where we are?" He assured me that we were on the right road to the regimental headquarters that he knew was just around the next bend. I looked behind us and a very frightening sight met my gaze. I saw what our frontlines looked like from the Chinese side! We had crossed through our frontlines, and we

An exhausted American infantryman rests after returning for a patrol in no man's land. Even though he is behind friendly lines, he has kept his steel helmet on and has his weapon handy. Most combat troops in Korea learned to sleep whenever they had the opportunity.

A 105-mm. howitzer of Battery B in a high angle fire position. This method of firing allowed the weapon to attack targets at the base of the reverse slope of the enemy's front. The projectile traveled almost straight up and then came down the same way. Many targets that were safe from low angle attack could be reached by high angle fire. However, the projectile was in the air for so long a time in high angle fire that it was less accurate than low angle fire.

were among the dug-in soldiers of the Chinese Army. I told O'Reilly to turn around, and he started to argue with me. I became very stern, and told him in no uncertain terms that we were in enemy territory. Finally, I got through to him.

He wheeled the little jeep around, and we started back to our lines post haste. I expected to hit a mine any second or that some Chinese soldier would begin shooting a sub-machine gun at us. Luckily, we made it back in one piece, and found our way to regimental headquarters. I never slept again when going to the front. I learned my lesson, and so did O'Reilly. We learned never to take a road unless we knew precisely where it led.

As long as I live, I will never forget what the American lines looked like from the Chinese side. I count myself to be lucky that I was not snapped up with O'Reilly and transported to a prisoner of war cage. The Good Lord had us by the hand that day.

CHAPTER 16

WHITE HORSE MOUNTAIN

Our RCT moved over on the right flank of the division to occupy a mountain known as White Horse Mountain. It was a rather large hill, which had been occupied by the South Korean Army before we moved in to relieve them. There were extensive trench systems on that hill, and we found out the hard way why the Koreans were so eager to give it to us to occupy in the early springtime.

There had been very hard fighting on that hill during the winter months. The Chinese had used their "mass attack" tactics on the South Koreans, trying to overrun them. In the process American artillery, my battalion included, had given heavy supporting fire to the South Koreans. The Chinese suffered heavy casualties, and were driven off of the hill leaving hundreds of their dead. It being in the coldest part of winter, the bodies of the Chinese soon became frozen. The South Koreans moved scores of those frozen bodies into their lines and used them as "filling" for the parapets they constructed in front of their trenches.

That tactic seemed to work well, that is until the thaw came. Our RCT relieved the South Koreans just as the temperature raised above freezing. I was at the front with one of our observers when a large mortar round struck nearby, shaking the ground. A part of the parapet near the trench we occupied gave away, and the foot of a dead Chinese soldier was exposed.

From a foxhole Captain Joseph Don Garrison, Jr., the brother of the author, looks across no man's land toward the forbidding enemy frontlines in Korea. The sharp parallel ridgeline in the center-right of the photograph is the distinctive Alligator Jaws known to all Thunderbirds who served in Korea. Note that the winter snows of 1951-1952 have almost melted and the spring of 1952 is approaching.

An American howitzer set up for high angle fire. A stockpile of shells is stacked on boxes to the left of the weapon ready for instant use. Note the laundry hung out to dry in the upper left of the photograph. It was difficult to stay clean on the Korean frontlines, especially during the wet season, but the cannoneers did the best they could.

The infantrymen examined the rest of the fortifications on the hill, and found they had all been built up through the use of frozen Chinese bodies. As the thaw became more complete, conditions became more untenable. Finally, the entire front-line was moved some feet behind the fortifications that had been built by the South Koreans. The infantry had to do a lot of digging, but they were glad to be out of that putrid area they had inherited. Funny people, those Koreans.

At the base of that hill I saw one of the most horrifying sights of my Korean service. As we drove the jeep toward the mountain, we came upon two GIs who were setting up a large flame throwing apparatus at its base. The way it worked was that a large container of jellied gasoline was at the bottom of the hill and a large and lengthy hose was taken to the top. That way, the defenders could refill the container from the base of the hill, and the soldiers at the top of the hill could spout flames from the nozzle on the end of the hose on any attacking force.

Somehow the hose became clogged. The two GIs who were setting up the weapon were working to unclog the thing. Something went wrong, and the whole reservoir of jellied gasoline blew up, mortally wounding one soldier and horribly burning the other one. I helped to cover those poor soldiers with army blankets, and their suffering has never once left my memory. The survivor was flown back to the States and taken to San Antonio, Texas, and placed in the Burn Center of the Army at Fort Sam Houston. He spent the rest of his life there. After the war I had occasion to be in Fort Sam Houston for reserve training, and I heard about that fellow. I toyed with the idea of going to see him, but I thought better of it. I did not want to relive that day, and I am sure he did not either. Undoubtedly, he is gone now, and I wonder about the way he must have suffered. "War," as Major General William T. Sherman said, "Is Hell." Sherman was certainly right about that. That was a long war for the poor burned GI.

CHAPTER 17

AN UNFORGETTABLE FRIEND

One cold December day, just after we had taken over from Battery B of the 77th Field Artillery Battalion of the First Cavalry Division, a column of trucks bearing the Infantrymen of the Eighth Cavalry Regiment of that division came along the road in front of our battery. A sergeant jumped off one of the trucks with a small figure in fatigue clothing and walked up to my battery command post. The sergeant had with him a little Korean boy who he introduced to our first sergeant as "Cheesi." That name means "small" in Japanese. The Japanese had occupied Korea for 55 years before the end of World War II, and a lot of their language had drifted over into the Korean language. He said that Cheesi was a fine house boy, who knew how to keep the oil stoves filled in our dugout, and could carry water and supplies to our "hoochie" that was our dugout hole in the side of a hill in the battery area. Cheesi was a fine looking little guy, and clean as a pin. He had obviously been well liked by his former comrades in the Eighth Cavalry, and they wanted to find him a good home before they left for Japan. I told the first sergeant that I would be glad to have his services as a houseboy, and there started one of the best friendships I have ever known.

Cheesi was, indeed, from a very high-class Korean family. As I got to know him better, he told me that his mother and father had been professors at the University of Seoul before the war started. When the Communist North Koreans came to the school, they took the entire faculty out to the banks of the Han River, and shot them to death. That day, Cheesi became an orphan. He was befriended by the GIs of the Eighth Cavalry who brought him to us.

That little guy was wonderful. Always cheerful and jovial, he would teach me a few words of Korean and then laugh at my mispronunciations. His Korean name was Jong Hoon. I would call to him, "Jong Hoon ediwa shipshaw!" which meant "Come here quickly" in Korean. He would always come running and laughing at my Korean pronunciation. I have thought about that little orphan boy many times since I came home. I received letters from him for a while but I have not heard from him in years. I will bet he became a successful individual in Korea after he reached manhood.

Once I was going up front, and I asked him if he wanted to go up with me and my driver. He hesitatingly said "Yes," and as we started out I looked at him and realized that he was sobbing. He did not want to go up to the front. He said he had gone through too much and was fearful for his life. He hated and feared the enemy, and he knew how cruel and treacherous the North Koreans were. We quickly turned around and took him back "home" to the battery area. He thanked us profusely, and said he hoped we understood that he was deathly afraid of the front. He was only 14 years old then, and an orphan.

Captain Denzil D. Garrison and his Korean house boy, Jong Hoon, better known as Cheesi, which meant "small" in Japanese. Cheesi was inherited by Battery B from the Eighth Cavalry when the battery arrived in Korea and quickly became a favorite of the men.

As I stated earlier, when it came time for me to go home, I was transferred from my battery to the battalion fire direction center, where I was the Assistant S-3. We were fighting all night every night, firing thousands of rounds at the enemy. I would just collapse and sleep all day, getting ready for another night of fighting. I was shaken awake by my old driver, who brought Cheesi to see me before I left for home. He was very sad and shaken that I was leaving, and he told me I was the only family he had. He cried pitifully and clung to me. I was really moved by his devotion. I had a beautiful trench knife I had purchased back in Japan, and I gave it to him as a gift. I will bet that somewhere in Korea that knife is still kept as a souvenir. Once after I came home I got a beautiful box from Cheesi containing a black lacquered desk ornament with my name on it in Oriental type characters. I still have that ornament on my desk, and I think of Jong Hoon every time I look at it. I hope life has been good to him. He deserved that much.

CHAPTER 18

ARMED WITH DISCARDS

In many ways, the Korean War turned into a very expensive undertaking for the United States. Millions of troops passed through that cauldron before it was over, and many still serve there, even today. One way our government tried to reduce the costs of the war was through the rehabilitation of equipment that had been left all over the Pacific at the end of World War II. Much equipment was just abandoned on many an island when the GIs were sent home. That is understandable, because it would have cost more to transport all that equipment home than to have just left it there where it was when victory was won.

The Army logisticians came up with a very novel plan on saving a lot of money. Units were sent from island to island across the Pacific Ocean looking for equipment and ammunition that could be salvaged and perhaps repaired for use in Korea. Astoundingly, Ordinance Corps people set up plants in Japan and began to recondition trucks, tanks, and artillery ammunition, among other things, that had been found where they had been abandoned at the end of World War II. All in all, I think it was a successful program in most cases. If the reconditioned equipment broke down, they would just send another one up. This worked particularly well with wheeled vehicles. It was not all that successful where the artillery ammunition was involved.

Artillery ammunition is complex. To improve accuracy, the ammunition is manufactured by powder lots. Where possible, we tried to use ammunition with the same powder lot for the day's shooting, to increase accuracy. The ammunition that came from all over the Pacific was not usually segregated by powder lot, and this diminished the accuracy of our fire. We just had to do the best we could with what we had. Artillery ammunition was very expensive, even during World War II. We were told at the Artillery School that a 105-mm. round of fuse quick, high explosive cost a $75 War Bond. A shell for a155-mm. cost twice as much. By the time the Korean War came along, the cost was even greater.

But the worst thing about those shells that came off the Pacific battlegrounds of World War II was the corrosion which had set in on the brass shell casings, many of which had even turned green. Some of the casings were bent. These had to be forced into the breech of the weapon. That condition caused the first battle casualties in our battery.

On 14 January 1952, we were assigned our regular missions of firing harassing and interdiction fire throughout the night. This fire was usually done by only one howitzer, and a single round, usually, would be fired into suspected areas of enemy activity on a schedule set up by the fire direction center. These missions kept the enemy awake, and I am sure some casualties were caused by this fire from time to time. At three in the morning the Number One howitzer crew

The Han River at Seoul, South Korea. Cheesi's parents were professors at the University of Seoul. When the North Koreans overran Seoul at the outbreak of the Korean War in the summer of 1950. Cheesi's parents and other faculty members were herded to the banks of the Han River and executed. At the time Cheesi was 12 years old.

Bill Mauldin became known world wide for his cartoons depicting the life of members of the 45th Infantry Division in World War II. One of his most famous cartoons showed an old army first sergeant of cavalry administering the "coup de grace" to his jeep. Much of the equipment received from the First Cavalry Division by the Thunderbirds in Korea was in sorrowful shape. In this photograph First Lieutenant Ed Saunders prepares to follow the cavalry first sergeant's lead by administering the "coup de grace" to his jeep that had been left behind by the First Cavalry Division.

attempted to load the shell into the breech of their weapon. The brass casing was so corroded that it would not fit into the tube. This crew had a very difficult time with a lot of those shells, and they kept a piece of wood handy to beat the shell casing home into the breech. Somehow, the propellant bags in the shell casing were set off before the breech was closed. That sent shards of brass flying all over the gun pit, severely wounding two of my men. Sergeant William R. Epps of McAlester, Oklahoma, was wounded about the face and head, and lost his eyesight, which was saved by medical treatment in the hospital in Japan. Another soldier, Private First Class Milton K. Daily, of Lebanon, Oregon, lost an arm. He too was evacuated to Japan. We never saw either of them again. They were both good soldiers, and I remember that Daily held frequent prayer sessions for his comrades, praying for their well being. It was a strange twist that he was one of the first to be wounded.

On the left is Corporal Norman Paterson of Elgin, Illinois, and on the right is First Lieutenant Edward Saunders, of Yonkers, New York. They were members of one of Battery B's forward observer parties on the frontlines in Korea. Paterson was a draftee and Saunders was a reserve officer who had served in Europe in World War II before being recalled to active duty for Korea. Note the fur-lined winter weather cap worn by Paterson. The cold weather clothing was necessary because of the crude living conditions on the frontlines during the harsh Korean winters.

It was so bitterly cold that night, and their wounds did not bleed because the blood froze when it hit the air. First Lieutenant Edgar J. Bradshaw, the battery executive officer, was in the battery fire direction center where he usually slept. He called for an ambulance, and medics were there in fairly short order. We met them out on the road and guided them to the gunpit involved. Bradshaw accomplished this task with efficiency. He was a very dependable officer and not easily excited. He acquitted himself very well that night.

The projectile, that is the shell itself, only traveled about half way up the tube. There was not sufficient propellant to eject the shell from the end of the tube. The howitzer remained that way until late the next day. Then our colonel, the "Old Maid," decided he would clear the tube. He had us rig up a very long lanyard, which is a rope used to trip the trigger that fires the round out of the tube. We got a 50-foot rope and tied it to the firing mechanism. Then the colonel got very deep in a foxhole, and after clearing all the troops away from the weapon he pulled the lanyard. The weapon had been pointed at a low mountain in front of the battery, and with a low powder charge the projectile exploded on the side of the unoccupied mountain. Inspection of the weapon showed that it was not harmed, and that day it was again firing on the enemy. We had suffered our first battle casualties due to this incident. They would not be our last.

CHAPTER 19

A QUIET HERO

Second Lieutenant Frank Fleet was not your everyday image of a warrior. Quiet and serious, he had very little to say sometimes. He certainly was not a braggart of any sort. He was assigned as forward observer with Battery A in our battalion. His small stature and almost timid approach did not lead anyone to suspect that under that facade was a combat competitor.

Once over on the north end of our sector in front of White Horse Mountain, Frank spotted an estimated 3,000 Chinese soldiers forming up in the open in preparation for a mass assault on our lines. That had never happened in our sector before, and Fleet grabbed the telephone and cranked open a connection with the battalion fire direction center.

He correctly reported that there were 3,000 Chinese infantrymen massed on the floor of the valley before our infantry preparing for a mass attack. He called for all available firepower on this, the best of all targets. Back at the fire direction center, the S-3 was incredulous. He said, "Now lieutenant, take another look at that and give us a correct report. What makes you think there are 3,000 Chinese there in the open, in broad daylight, waiting to attack our dug-in front-line?" Fleet was insistent, but still the major did not give him the fire he asked for. Fleet, usually noncommittal, became more excited and screamed into the telephone that a mass attack was indeed about to commence.

Finally, another observer down the line picked up the same target, and breathlessly reported that thousands of the enemy were massing to attack our lines. At last Fleet was vindicated. The major realized that something very big was about to happen out in front of our infantry.

Far overhead a flight of huge B-50 bombers lumbered into North Korea armed with anti-personnel bombs scheduled for the often-bombed North Korean Officers School up around Pyongyang, the capitol of North Korea. A forward air controller with our infantry contacted the flight and alerted them to the situation. He pinpointed the target area, and the bombers came in together at about 500 feet in altitude. The enemy was caught in the open.

The awful destruction of that enemy regiment by those deadly fragmentation bombs will never be forgotten by those who saw it among the Chinese or the Americans. The Chinese regiment was almost totally destroyed by the red-hot splinters from the anti-personnel bombs. Soon, there were no more targets to punish. That defeat was the most complete and one-sided we ever handed out to the enemy in Korea. Thousands of Chinese were lost, and the Americans suffered not one casualty. We often wondered what stupid Chinese commander ordered that mass attack when and where he did.

Frank Fleet was the first to spot that attack coming. He practically had to beg for fire to be brought on one of the most inviting targets of the war. From that day on he was regarded in a different light in our outfit. He did not need to take a back seat to anyone. I was proud of him, and I am honored to call him my friend. He turned out to be quite a warrior after all.

CHAPTER 20

HUMOR AT THE FRONT

Looking back over my service, I remember many things and people. Some of those things are still sad in my memory, and some are hilariously funny to me. One of the true wits I have ever known was Captain Paschel M. Huff of the 180th Infantry Regiment.

Huff started out as a company commander and ended up as a member of the First Battalion staff as the S-2. The S-2 was the intelligence officer, and it was his job to keep up on enemy plans and operations. Usually, the S-2 was a little different cut than the other officers of the line units. That was certainly true of Huff. The mold was broken after he was made. There never was a wittier man, and his sparkling repartee was ready anywhere, anytime. He saw humor in most all circumstances, and he loved to poke holes in bloated egos. As a matter of fact he was an expert at that.

My brother, Joseph Don Garrison, Jr., was an S-2 in the 179th Infantry Regiment, and he had gone to Intelligence School with Huff. He first told me what a character Paschel Huff was. When I came to know Huff in Korea, he lived up to his advanced billing.

The bane of all the S-2s in the division was the division G-2, who took that assignment just as we entered Korea. He quickly became known as "Luke the Spook." Luke worked mightily to keep track of Chinese capabilities, but, alas, he came up against a hard task. Keeping Huff in line became almost a mania with him. Huff knew this, and he carried on a duel of wits for months with Luke the Spook, and he always won.

On the left is Captain Paschel Huff and on the right is Captain Stanley Stone, both members of the 180th Infantry Regiment. Paschel is wearing cotton fatigues beneath his field jacket. Stone is wearing a wool uniform underneath his field jacket. The troops in Korea were equipped with both types of uniforms.

Our tank battalion, the 245th, had lost several tanks out in no-man's land to mines, which had knocked their tracks off. Nightfall came before the tank retrievers could reach the damaged tanks to bring them in. Everyone watched the hulks, knowing that the Chinese would be poking around them come nightfall.

Sure enough, about two hours after dark, a Chinese patrol came upon the derelicts and soon they were burning. This report went back to division, and finally into the hands of Luke the Spook. Luke looked on the situation map, and saw that these tanks were in the area of the

front held by the First Battalion, 180th Infantry Regiment, which was Huff's outfit. Without further delay, Luke called to the switchboard of the First Battalion asking for Captain Huff, who was snoozing away in his bedroll safe in a dugout.

"Huff," said Luke, "There are a group of knocked out friendly tanks out to your left front. They are burning. I want an intelligence report on them at once." Huff asked him what he wanted to know about those tanks. Luke said, "I want a complete report. Find out who burned the tanks, and why, and what they used to fuel the fire." Huff, never getting out of bed, said, "I'll be back with that information quickly, sir." He then turned over and tried to get in a little rest before the report was made. After a while, Huff rang up the switchboard and asked for Luke. Presently Luke answered, and Huff reported, "Sir, several Orientals of unknown name or origin, stealthily sneaked up and set fire to those tanks. My investigation bore out the fact that they used a Zippo cigarette lighter." Luke retorted, "Very well, keep me informed."

How Huff kept from being stood at attention by Luke is a wonder, but he did. His exploits in regard to Luke became legendary in the division.

Another time, a Chinese patrol came close to our lines and set off colored rockets, all the while blowing bugles. We never knew if they did those things to frighten us, or to control the actions of their troops. Because their radio equipment was archaic and scarce, in all probability they were using visual and sound methods to control the movement of their units maneuvering across the front. On one particular night in the spring of 1952, hand-held rocket flares were sent into the air and bugles sounded. That always put everyone on edge.

Huff on the other hand was in bed again. The phone rang, and Huff was awakened. "Yes," he said, "How can I help you?" Luke identified himself, and told Huff about the rocket flares and the bugle calls. He said, "I want to know where those rockets came from, where they went, and what became of them. I also want to know who blew the bugle, if you can find out." Huff again said he would look into the matter and call back. He laid the phone down and after a sufficient time he rang Luke back up. He said, "Colonel those rocket flares started out from the ground, and went up. Some were red, and some were green. They went up for some time then they seemed to stop. Then, they came down again to the ground. As to the bugle, one report has it that it was blown by Louie Armstrong, but that has not been confirmed. I believe it was blown by a member of the Chinese Army."

How Huff ever got away with such shenanigans is a mystery. As he used to say, however, "The worst Luke can do to me is to send me to Korea, and I am already there!"

CHAPTER 21

WINNING A DEADLY DUEL

As a graduate of the Artillery School at Fort Sill, I came to be almost addicted to the adjustment of artillery fire. That may sound crazy, but there is a real art to using artillery, and I have to admit that we became very adept at hitting targets at long distances. I used to enjoy going up to be with our forward observers, and I always gave a shot or two to the enemy while I was there.

Once, I was in an observation post on Hill 234, a part of our MLR, and we spotted a Chinese observer across the valley. He was using field glasses just as we were, adjusting the huge 160-mm. mortars they used so well. Soon, the explosions of the mortar shells landed very near to our bunker, and we realized that the Chinese observer was shooting directly at us! We took up the challenge with alacrity.

That Chinese officer with the glasses was standing in a V-shaped opening in their trench, showing about the upper third of his body. Seeing this, we called in precision fire from our fire direction center on the trench where we saw the observer. The howitzer is a weapon with a rather slow muzzle velocity, and its projectiles travel up quite a way before they start down. This resulted in a situation where the Chinese observer could hear our howitzer shoot long before the shell arrived. He would just drop down into the bunker under the V-shaped opening whenever he heard the howitzer fire, and then he would show up again and shoot a round or two at us from the huge mortar. Soon we knew we were in a duel of forward observers, and we had to figure a way to win.

The infantry platoon leader, First Lieutenant Harold Hampton was there with me as the duel progressed. He had a direct line into a tank that was dug into the mountain about 100 yards down the line. We rang up the tanker and explained our problem. He spotted the Chinese observer when we pointed out his V-shaped position to him. We decided that the tanker should try to adjust in on the V at the same time as our next round landed. When the next howitzer round landed, another round from the 76-mm. gun of the tank landed also. We repeated this little trick, and the tank gunner told us after observing his round strike, that the next tank shell would land squarely in the V. We told him to load up and shoot at our command.

Then we ordered another round from our howitzer. We heard it being fired, as did the Chinese observer. He almost nonchalantly ducked back into his dugout, and quickly started back up into the V when our round had landed. Just as the top of his head appeared, we ordered to the tank, "Fire!" It took only a fraction of a second for that high velocity tank shell to cross the valley. By the time the Chinese

A forward observer team of Battery B on the frontlines. Left to right, Sergeant Donald J. Stacy, Private First Class Jerry T. McElroy, and First Lieutenant Giles Crisler. Because they were stationed on the frontline and therefore subject to enemy attacks, forward observer duty was the most dangerous for member of Battery B.

observer had stood up, the tank projectile arrived in the V. It hit him directly in the chest, and blew him to bits. We had won the duel, but we were not all that enthused about it.

In one of the strange coincidences that happened from time to time, I was surprised to run into Harold Hampton years after the war in Bartlesville, Oklahoma, where I had established my law practice. I called to him on the street, and he immediately recognized me. We reminisced about the Chinese observer and our long duel with him. One thing we knew, that Chinese observer had not made it back home as we had done.

Looking out over no man's land from the American observation post on Hill 347. Another observation post was maintained on Hill 323 on the left side of the photograph. This photograph was made early in the spring of 1952. Note the smoke in the center of the photograph coming from a fire on the communist side of the frontlines.

CHAPTER 22

ONE LEAK TOO MANY

The long-range duels we had across the valleys between our lines and the enemy's were fascinating in many ways. Both sides were looking for prisoners at all times. A lot could be found out from a prisoner, which could turn out to be helpful in future skirmishes. We tried a lot of things to take some prisoners, mostly to no avail. Finally, the theater intelligence officers came up with a plan that was doomed to failure before it really started.

At a time certain, 8:00 a.m. on a certain morning, all artillery harassing and interdiction fire ceased along with all attacks from artillery spotter planes, and even the Air Force. No attacks were to be mounted from infantry mortars, and the entire front was to become quiet for a full week.

The idea was that the enemy would become curious and step up his patrolling activity pushing closer and closer to our lines, and finally, we hoped, we could surprise and ensnare an entire patrol. There was only one drawback. The Chinese and North Koreans had excellent intelligence coming from Korean agents working and living within our lines, and they knew the exact time the "quiet time" was to start and end. This made the whole plan something of a farce.

At 8:05 a.m. on the first morning the enemy started strolling about his front-lines, paying little attention to us, other than to look over and wave once in a while. This was most infuriating to us who sat across the valley with overwhelming firepower at our disposal and orders not to use it. As a matter of fact, no guns were to be fired except on the order of the division commander. This helped the Chinese, and certainly did nothing for us. The entire plan was a blunder, which operated to play into the enemy's hands.

Joe Hendrix, a close friend of mine, was a forward observer from Battery "C," 171st F.A. battalion, in our battalion. He was stationed with the infantry when the infamous cease-fire went into effect. Joe watched the Chinese positions closely through his powerful BC Scope, which was set up in his observation post. He spotted something of interest just minutes after quiet time went into effect.

A Chinese officer stepped out into the open shortly after dawn, walked across an open stretch to a scrubby tree and urinated on it. He looked around at the beginning of a beautiful day, knowing he would not be shot at while relieving himself so leisurely. This infuriated Joe. He calculated the exact coordinates of that scrubby tree, and sent them back to the fire direction center. At the FDC, another observer

An infantry command post with the sandbagged walls reinforced with logs. Although it probably would not survive a direct hit from heavy artillery, it afforded protection from most enemy weapons. Note the hand rails beside the path on the lower left. The rails and the gravel put on the path allowed men to make it up and down the steep hill during wet weather when the hillside turned to mud.

A photograph of Battery B's firing position. The 105-mm. howitzer with smoke coming from its barrel has just fired. Note the earth embankment around the howitzer and the supply trucks to provide protection from enemy fire.

was contacted down the line that also located the tree from his map. Every known method of preparing firing data to hit that tree was used. And each morning, the Chinese officer went to the same tree for the same purpose at the same time. He seemed to be taunting us. It certainly seemed that way to Joe Hendrix.

Finally, on the last day of the quiet time the Chinese officer again sauntered over to the tree for his usual ritual. He had underestimated Joe Hendrix. Joe had explained the whole situation to the S-3 of division artillery, and the S-3 had gotten permission to fire one round before the quiet time was to end. An artillery metro message was used to get corrections for the guns to use to improve accuracy. The howitzer was loaded and waiting when the Chinese officer went to do his morning social. As he reached the tree and began to urinate on it, the weapon fired. Although the chances of hitting that tree were not good at all, this time was the exception. The 105-mm. round hit right at the feet of the Chinese officer. That was his last leak, so to speak. All who had watched this develop for the preceding week broke into a loud cheer. For once, we got the last laugh.

What was so surprising about this was that the corrections obtained for the weapon based on a metro message were notoriously inaccurate. It was common knowledge among artillerymen that "Metro message data is such that if you hit your target based on it, you know that you made a mistake in your figures!" If that was the thinking of the Chinese officer involved, he certainly made a mistaken calculation. What a way and what a time to die!

CHAPTER 23

THE CRATER

One of the most disagreeable things about the Korean War was the weather. The frozen and ice-covered ground of the winter was replaced by the choking dust of the Korean summer. Although I hated the dust that permeated everything and everybody, still it did not measure up to the bone-chilling blasts of the ice-laden wind blowing down from Siberia. That cold was the worst, without a doubt.

We had a master sergeant named Edgar Conn, who was known by everyone in the outfit as "Boodle." Where that name came from is a mystery to me, but they all called him that. He was a blustering fellow, and it took a lot of knowing to like him. At first he struck one as being a loud-mouthed braggart, but slowly it dawned on a person that there were a lot of things to like about him.

One thing about Boodle Conn, he was ready to try anything. Assign him a job, and he would give it a try. He was a jack-of-all trades, knowing just a little bit about a lot of things. He volunteered to dig that new gun pit through the ice in a hurry. He was going to use

On the left is Colonel Frederick A. Daughtery, commander of the 179th Infantry Regiment. On the right is Lieutenant Colonel William E. Murphy the commander of the First Battalion, 179th Infantry Regiment in Korea. Colonel Murphy was an excellent infantry commander, who served with the 45th Division in Italy, France, and Germany in World War II. His experience and leadership made him one of the best infantry battalion commanders in Korea.

explosives to do the job. We only had two sticks of dynamite in the battery, and he said that was enough. His plan was to blow a small pilot hole in the ice with the dynamite, and then to fill that hole with unused powder bags from the howitzers. That was a commodity we had plenty of. Each round of 105-mm. ammunition had seven powder charges contained in the canister. Because most of our shooting at that position was using charge five, that left two unused powder bags for each round fired.

The pilot hole took the better part of a day to dig. Finally, the dynamite was exploded in the bottom of it, and a hole in a "light-bulb" shape, about three and a half feet deep, was formed. This hole Boodle filled with powder bags from the guns. That looked like an awful lot of explosives to me, but Boodle assured me that it was a low grade explosive which would not make much of a bang at all.

The hole was filled by dark, and it was agreed that the explosion would take place the next morning. The sun rose, and the entire battery gazed at the pilot hole and wondered. Finally, Boodle hooked up the detonator to the explosive, and I luckily moved all the men a safe distance away, I thought.

"Fire in the hole," Boodle screamed, and then he pressed on the detonator. There was a tremendous explosion. Smoke erupted from the hole, and finally cleared away enough so that we could see in the gaping chasm. What a sight we saw. There in the middle of the battery was a hole 20 feet deep and 45 feet wide. It was a huge excavation at least four times as deep and three times as wide as we needed to serve as a gun pit for one of our howitzers. Boodle said, "Oh hell, I used too much powder!" The Crater, as we named it, was useless for any purpose we could think of. Boodle grinned and said, "We can prove that we've been bombed, now!"

The key personnel of Battery B's fire direction center were, left to right, Sergeant Walter V. Allison, Warrant Officer Ernest McKean, First Lieutenant Edgar Bradshaw, Master Sergeant Herbert L. Tash, Master Sergeant James A. Nolan, and Sergeant First Class John L. Cloyd. All of the men were from McAlester, Oklahoma, or surrounding towns.

Four stalwarts of Battery B, 171st Field Artillery. Left to right: Sergeant First Class Samuel T. Bullard, Sergeant First Class Floyd K. Clark, Master Sergeant Edgar J. "Boodle" Conn, and First Sergeant John Dunn. Note that Boodle Conn has removed his steel helmet just to be different from the rest. It would be hard to find better men anywhere. It was Conn who used unused powder bags in an attempt to blast a gun pit in the frozen ground. Unfortunately the explosion blew a huge hole much to deep for a gun pit.

Several months later we were replaced by a battery from another unit that took over our sector. I heard one of the men in the new outfit ask one of my men, “How in the hell did you get that huge hole right in middle of the battery position?” My man looked at him and said, “This is a rough sector. That is a shell hole from one of the Chinese’s bigger artillery pieces.” The apprehensive soldier said, “This is a tough sector ain’t it?”

When we remonstrated with Boodle about the chasm he had created, he just grinned and said he would know more about the use of explosives next time. He gave us his usual Irish grin, and we had to laugh. He is gone now, with too many of his comrades. I can just hear him volunteering for all sorts of tasks, wherever he may be! As he was often reminded, “A jack-of-all-trades is the master of none.”

CHAPTER 24

A NEW FRIEND

There was one stretch of road in the northern portion of our sector that was treacherous to use. It was a road leading over the very top of a hill within full view of the Chinese observation posts across the valley, and under direct fire of Chinese 76-mm. field artillery pieces.

The 76-mm. used by the Chinese was not a howitzer; it was a gun, which meant that it had a flat trajectory rather than the "curved" trajectory of the howitzer. This made the 76-mm. practically useless as an area weapon, such as the 105-mm. howitzer we used. But it was deadly as an accurate weapon used in direct fire. The howitzer, on the other hand, could and did shoot at targets over mountains and thousands of yards away, and entire battalions of them could be massed on one target. The 76-mm. gun of the Chinese was hardly ever used with other 76-mm. guns to mass fire. As a matter of fact, I do not remember a single time I ever saw Chinese or North Korean artillery massed as we did ours.

But used singly, the high velocity 76-mm. gun of the Chinese Army could be deadly. They used it as one would fire a rifle, sighting a target directly from the weapon, and shooting one aimed round at a time. The enemy usually kept at least one 76-mm. gun trained on one particular pass crossing a hill we occupied in full view of their gunners.

The sandbagged bunker on the left of the photograph was used by First Lieutenant Edward Saunders, a forward observer for Battery B, for protection from enemy fire. Unlike most bunkers it was not deeply dug into the ground. Although this left Saunders more exposed it allowed him to keep the enemy lines under direct observation while calling in artillery fire. The sandbags did provide protection from small arms fire and shell fragments.

A 105-mm. howitzer of Battery B that has just fired and is in full recoil. The gunner has the telephone to his ear to take the next fire command from the fire direction center. Unfortunately, the gunner is violating standing orders by not wearing his steel helmet, which could save his life in the event of a muzzle burst. The wheels of the howitzer have been placed on a wooden platform to keep it from sinking in the mud during wet weather. On the left a supply of shells is stored beneath a canvas cover.

Lieutenant General LaVern E. Weber, who the author met in a shell crater on the frontlines in Korea, when they were both captains. They remained close friends for all their days. In ensuing years, Lieutenant General Weber became the Chief of the National Guard Bureau in Washington, D. C. He was a fine soldier.

One day in early 1952, I was traveling over that pass going to visit one our observers that was with the infantry. As we entered the danger area, a 76-mm. round missed our jeep by inches. I can still feel the rush of that projectile which sailed past to explode several hundred yards behind us.

We knew that the next round would hit us for sure, and we drove the jeep into a ravine, where we were surprised to see another jeep sitting. We "bailed out" and dived into a large bomb crater next to the road. In the bottom of the crater were an infantry captain and his driver. I sheepishly grinned to him and introduced myself. He stated that he was LaVern Weber of the infantry. He said he had been in that hole for two hours, and showed me his hands which were filled with sweat. We both laughed nervously at that and wondered what to do next. He put his helmet on his carbine, and held it up to the top of the hole. Almost at once, a 76-mm. shell was fired barely missing our hole. We were in a hell of a mess.

Captain Weber asked me if I was related to Captain Garrison of the infantry. I told him I was Captain Garrison's brother. As the day wore on, we became closer and closer friends. We stayed in that hole till it became dark, then we executed "Howe Able."

LaVern Weber and I were friends thereafter. I was happy to be instrumental in the appointment of LaVern Weber as Adjutant General of the State of Oklahoma by Governor Henry Bellmon, in later years. As such, he became a major general. Later, he became the Chief of the National Guard Bureau with the rank of lieutenant general. He is one of only a very few Oklahomans to reach that high rank. Both General Weber and former Oklahoma Governor Bellmon had been Marines in World War II. They hit it off famously through the years. Whenever I saw Weber, he always asked me if I had been shot into any holes in the ground lately. We always laughed about that, but neither of us would want to go through it again. He lost his life in a tragic accident on his farm a short time ago. Oklahoma lost one of her best sons when that happened. He was a real soldier and a loyal friend.

Which goes to show you that you never know whom you will meet in a bomb crater. It behooves one to keep that in mind.

CHAPTER 25

A NARROW ESCAPE

My brother, who was an infantry officer during World War II, had some very sound ideas on how to stay alive in a war. He had learned them the hard way. He was a captain over in the infantry, and there were plenty of ways to "buy the farm" there, without volunteering. He always said, "Don't go anywhere you haven't been ordered to go, and don't volunteer for anything." He had not always followed that path himself, having been decorated in Europe for allowing the Germans to shoot at him in order to locate an 88-mm. gun they were firing. I almost cashed in my chips when I violated those axioms, in the spring of 1951.

I had the best job in the Army, according to all the old soldiers I had listened to during my time in the military. I was a battery commander in the field artillery, and that was supposed to be the top assignment in the walking Army. As an old battery commander, President Harry Truman once described the job, "Any damn fool can be an artillery battery commander, if he has a good first sergeant." As I have already said, I had the best first soldier of them all. It was pretty difficult to get killed as a battery commander, but I almost succeeded in doing that very thing.

One of my lieutenants was Bill Sumter, who was also one of my best friends. He was detailed back to the division artillery air section as an aerial artillery observer. He genuinely loved that assignment, for it was a long way from our "old maid" battalion commander. He loved the flying, and he flew at least four hours every day. I secretly envied his duty, and I sneaked back to the rear to see him a lot. I liked being around the pilots and planes, and to have the flying and the artillery meshed into one job seemed to be a dream assignment to me.

Sumter had one thing we all coveted. He had a color portrait of Mitzi Gaynor, the actress, all dressed up in a pair of short-shorts just dancing away. We all admired Mitzi and the picture, which we ogled every chance we got.

On this particular day in the Korean springtime, Sumter was not feeling too well. As a matter of fact he had a hell of a hangover, which was not too unusual for him or any of the rest of us for that matter. He begged me, "Please take my flight for me today. My head feels like a piano has been dropped on it."

Seeing that I had him at a disadvantage, I said, "I'll take the flight for you if you'll give me the picture of Mitzi Gaynor." He said in no uncertain terms that he would never do that, and started to get off his cot. His head hurt so much that he fell back on the bed. He said, "Garrison, you are taking unfair advantage of me, but I don't have any choice. Take the picture, you rat!"

I took the revered picture out of its frame and put it in my map case. I felt like I had made a very good deal. I had only to take a long flight up and down the frontlines, and Mitzi would be mine forever. It never occurred to me that I might run into trouble during that flight.

The liaison planes used by artillery outfits in the Korean War were little Cessnas known as L-19s. They held two people in tandem. That is, the pilot sat in the front seat and the observer sat in the back seat.

I loved to adjust artillery fire, especially from the air. It was a good deal like shooting fish in a rain-barrel, if you know what I mean. We had this capability, and our enemy did not. The Chinese detested those little planes because they had to stay hidden during all the hours of daylight. We would fly parallel to the frontlines, directing artillery fire at anything that moved. They hated those planes, and they fired at them any time they could.

The pilot I drew that day was Bill Cook (not his real name), a native of Alabama. We called him Amos Cook, because he talked like the characters in Amos and Andy, the radio show. Amos was not sure he had his heart in that war and he fortified himself with a considerable amount of beer both before and during flights. The beer filled him with plenty of "Dutch courage," if you follow me. At any rate, Amos was a lot more aggressive as the beer guzzling progressed. Flying high over the front kept the beer as cold as an icebox. This suited Amos just fine, although he flew too high for real effective shooting until the beer got really cold. Then he would go down and get with it.

We took off and went up and up. Amos carried his beer in a camera case, and it presently became frosty. Smiling, he started down to our task. All at once we heard a loud explosion and our little plane shook and sputtered a bit. Just below and behind us appeared an ugly black smoke cloud. We realized that we were being shot at. I took my field glasses and searched the lines below. The American side of the front was easily seen, covered by trucks, soldiers, and all sorts of equipment. On the Chinese side absolutely nothing could be seen, except miles and miles of trenches. Just then our adversaries cut loose with another round, which exploded just behind us. Out of the corner of my eye, I saw the gun from which these rounds came. It was on the very top of a hill, and its crew was gathered around it. I hurriedly opened up my map to identify the map coordinates of the weapon. Alas, I realized that the enemy gun was on a hill that my map did not cover. I motioned to Amos that we would have to go back down to get another map, and he nodded that he understood.

We headed back to the airstrip not knowing that our landing gear was damaged by those near misses. After we landed, I jumped out, got the proper new map showing the target hill, and quickly got back into the plane behind Amos. He gunned the little plane down the airstrip at full speed. About halfway down the strip, the landing gear, which the pilot later said was damaged by the enemy shells, collapsed. Amos tried to hold the nose up, but he could not. The L-19 veered off the runway, rose a few feet in the air, and flew through a squad tent full of GIs. Miraculously, none of those soldiers were killed, although several of them were hurt.

Our little plane lurched on through and past the tent, and careened

An Army L-19 (Birddog) Observation Plane on display at the 45th Infantry Division Museum in Oklahoma City, Oklahoma. The L-19 was not armored and carried a pilot in the front seat and an artillery observer in the rear seat. Although it could not deliver bombs or napalm, it still had a deadly sting. The artillery observer could deliver the entire fire of a division's artillery in minutes and as a result the enemy grew to respect this little plane. It was this type of aircraft that the author made his ill-fated flight over enemy lines in the spring of 1951.

into the most dreaded of all places to a combat soldier. We landed at the edge of a marked minefield, which had been laid as part of the defense of the airstrip. I shut my eyes and braced myself for the explosion I expected to come. My head struck a support bar at the top of the plane, knocking me partially unconscious. Amos crawled out of the plane, and did not turn the motor off. The propeller churned on, digging up great chunks of dirt. In my addled mind, I knew that fire could certainly result from that situation. The propeller might trip one of those wires that were concealed throughout the minefield, too.

Amos left me in the plane. The only thing he rescued was his camera case full of beer. He gingerly picked his way out of the minefield,

and turned to see the propeller still spinning. I was strapped in the plane, unable to get out.

Still groggy, I dimly saw a figure carefully coming toward me. I recognized Gene Short, an older officer in our outfit who had been overseas in many months of combat in World War II and Korea. He worked his way to me and turned off the switch on the control panel. The propeller at last ceased its churning. Slowly, and ever so tediously Gene guided me out of the minefield. Clutched in my hand was my map case, still containing the portrait of Mitzi Gaynor.

Amos then became solicitous of my well being, now that Gene Short had gotten me out of danger. He drawled, "Go right over and get in another plane, and we'll go back up. If we don't, we may be afraid to fly any more." Gene scowled at him and said, "He can go up in

Another type of aircraft successfully used by the Army in Korea was the medical evacuation helicopter, usually a modified H-5A such as this, which could transfer a wounded soldier from the frontlines to a field hospital in the rear in a matter of minutes. The rapid transport of wounded to hospitals saved many American lives in Korea.

another plane if he wants to, but you sure as hell won't be flying it!" I never took another flight in Korea. I never saw Amos again. But I have seen Gene many times. He is gone now, but I will always love him.

When I fully regained my senses, I was on a cot in a squad tent. Gene was bent over me. I said to him, "Thank you, friend. That's one I owe you." At the time, I did not know that it would be 18 years before I could repay him. But that is another story.

CHAPTER 26

CORRECTING AN ANCIENT MISTAKE

For the most part, the American military was not racially integrated until the Korean War. When we received our fillers in Louisiana, they were all white. I am sure this did not just happen. Someone up at the top was segregating the replacement pools. I do not remember the subject being discussed all that much, but it just seemed to have been the way things were done.

At this time, looking back, there is really no rational defense for the idea that somehow the two races, black and white, cannot serve together in integrated units. That has been disproved many times and in many ways. In our battery we handled the "problem" very successfully.

After we had been in Korea about a month, our first replacements arrived at battalion headquarters. The battalion adjutant called me and informed me that many of the replacements were black. Our battery was receiving its first black soldier in the shipment of replacement troops that were on the way up to the firing position. Being that Oklahoma was a state with quite a bit of Southern heritage, I did not know how this new soldier would be received by the men of the unit. Leadership was called for, and our first sergeant, John Dunn delivered it.

I shall never forget the meeting of the men of the battery there around the gun pit of the Number 3 Howitzer Section. The Native American first sergeant, speaking quietly, talked to the men in such a way that they really seemed to take his words to heart. He told them that we were to receive our first black replacement that day. He told them that the replacement would be treated with the respect he was due as an American soldier, and that he would not tolerate any sort of discrimination, of any type, against the new member of our battery. He stopped and looked straight into the eyes of those soldiers, and said, "Anyone who mistreats this new man will have me to answer to!" His words were clearly understood by all that heard them.

Shortly, the truck bearing the new replacements arrived. As I remember, there were five of them. One of the five was a small soldier from Texas, named Eddie Bell. He was very black and very nervous. The first sergeant personally took him to the gun crew with which he was to serve. He introduced Bell to his new comrades and to his new section leader. They all shook his hand and tried to make him feel as one of them. They were successful. Eddie Bell became one of the most popular men in the battery. I was thankful that he was well received. I know that this transition was easily made mainly because of the efforts of John Dunn, our first sergeant, and Eddie Bell, our newest replacement.

By the time I rotated home, the battery had 18 black soldiers on its roster, and we never had any problems in that regard. Integration had come to Battery B, and we certainly were not any the worse for it. As a matter of fact, we were proud of the fact that our efforts in that situation were successful.

The entire American military establishment in Korea had a lot of the same experience. We were too busy fighting a war to be distracted by Jim Crowism in carrying out our duties. Never again were our units segregated. This was one of the best things Harry Truman ever did as president. I did not agree with him in a lot of ways, but he was right to desegregate the armed forces. Since that time our military has been highly successful in integrating the various races and working together for the common good.

Private Eddie Bell standing beside one of Battery B's 105-mm howitzers. Korea was the American war in which racial segregation was ended in the military and Bell's addition to the unit broke "the color barrier." First Sergeant John Dunn personally took Bell to his gun crew and introduced him. With that, Bell was immediately accepted and eventually became one of the most popular men in the battery.

CHAPTER 27

A THUNDERBIRD HERO

One of the finest men I have ever known was Harry W. Hughes. He lived in Norman, the town of my boyhood. My father was superintendent of schools there. My father entered the service as a member of the 45th Infantry Division in 1940, and returned to the school job in 1946 after he left active duty. Dad had been a member of the Oklahoma National Guard in World War I, and served in France as a young corporal.

During the pre-war years, my father was the commander of Company D, 179th Infantry Regiment, which was a machine gun company in those days. One of his officers was a little meek second lieutenant named Harry Hughes. Harry was a devout Baptist, and he preached and followed the tenet that it was better to turn the other cheek.

Harry was my sixth-grade American history teacher. His quiet lessons were usually filled with patriotism, and that always pleased me. He was also the football coach, and I appreciated that a lot. In all the years I knew him, I never heard Harry curse or use vulgarity even one time. He would have been the last person in the world to be selected as a potential infantry war hero. As they say, you cannot always tell.

When the division was called to active duty in World War II, Harry still served with Company D. An old story, which has been told many times, concerned a boy who had been reared by strict Baptists who were close friends of Harry. This young soldier went out on the town

Lieutenant Colonel Harry W. Hughes, a battalion commander of the 179th Infantry in both Europe and Korea. A true hero, who suffered 44 puncture wounds in Europe. As fate would have it, he also was severely wounded in Korea by a "bouncing-betty" mine. He was in and out of military hospitals for three years after his Korean wounds.

in Abilene, Texas, where the division was training and was picked up by the MPs for being drunk and disorderly. Monday, the delinquency report arrived on Harry's desk, and he called the boy in. He said, "Jack, I have known you and your people most of your life, and I think you must have been influenced by some other person to do such a thing. Just who was it that influenced you, son?"

The young soldier, still suffering from a healthy hangover answered, "Hiram Walker, Sir." Harry, having led such a straight life did not recognize that as the name of a famous brand of bourbon whiskey. He said quickly, "What outfit is he in. I'll see that he doesn't lead any other good Christian boys astray!" That story was known to everyone in the company in short order. They must have wondered what kind of a combat leader Harry would make. They need not have worried.

The 45th Division landed in Sicily with Harry leading his company ashore. Little meek Harry Hughes was a tiger. He was always up at the very frontlines showing absolutely no fear for his own safety, and yet caring for his men the very best he could. Even in the midst of combat, no one ever heard Harry Hughes utter any oath or vulgarity. He was a gentleman even there.

Soon, he was wounded rather severely. Taken back to the hospital he was bandaged up and told to take a rest before they sent him back to his unit. Harry proceeded to leave the hospital surreptitiously and hitched a ride back to his unit. The medics were called and told that Harry was back up front. That happened not once, but several times. He became a legend in his own time. He was promoted again and again and became a lieutenant colonel and the battalion commander. He was wounded so many times that he suffered 44 different puncture wounds from enemy action in Sicily, Italy, and France. That was said to be the record in the United States Army. I never met anyone who approached that number of wounds, either in World War II or Korea. The worst was yet to come.

When the division was called to active duty in September of 1950, almost every officer who had stayed in the Regular Army after service with the 45th pulled every string possible to get sent back to the

Thunderbirds. As you might have guessed, Lieutenant Colonel Harry W. Hughes was one of the first to arrive.

Harry was assigned as a battalion commander in his old regiment, the 179th. He was back home. He trained that battalion as only he could, and his men knew him as a fearless and fair leader. They gave an excellent account of themselves when we arrived in combat up near Chorwon on the frontlines in North Korea.

On 5 May 1952 Harry was making a reconnaissance of a new position for his battalion. He left his driver in his jeep, and walked up a draw that looked as though it had never been occupied. It only looked that way. Harry walked several yards into the defile and stepped as lightly as he could in doing so. But this was his unlucky day; more unlucky than all the other days he had pressed his luck all over Europe. He stepped on the mine most dreaded by the infantry, a bouncing betty. This particular mine worked just as it was designed.

The explosion was directly in the face of Harry. His eyes were badly hurt, and every bone in his face was shattered. His chest was penetrated, and he was near death when he arrived at the hospital by the helicopter that came for him. In that war, by the way, helicopters for the most part were used only for the evacuation of wounded.

I was devastated when I heard about Harry's horrible wounds. No one expected him to survive such damage. I knew about his history, and I told my comrades that if any one could make it through such a thing it would be Harry Hughes.

Harry spent three years in and out of military hospitals after his 45th puncture wound. It was his last wound, and certainly his worst. His face was completely reconstructed. Luckily, his twin brother was a perfect copy of Harry, and the plastic surgeons had a model to follow. Slowly a reconstructed face appeared, looking a lot like Harry, but still not quite the same. The tear ducts in his eyes were blown away, and Harry seemed to be crying because tears were always falling from his eyes. He carried a supply of handkerchiefs with him always after he was finally retired from the Army. He was still the perfect gentleman he had always been, and he lived the same spotless life he had always known. Everyone respected and loved him, as they always had. He is the most unforgettable character most of us had ever known.

I served once again with Harry on the Board of Directors of the Oklahoma Historical Society. He still loved history, and he enjoyed his service on that board immensely.

After all those wounds, Harry died a tragic death when struck by a school bus as he drove in Lawton, Oklahoma. When I heard about the accident, I drove immediately to the hospital in Lawton, and went to his side. He recognized me, and we spoke a few words together for the last time. A day later, one of America's greatest heroes died. He did not curse, did not run around, did not drink, but he was one of the real men I have ever known.

CHAPTER 28

THE HOME FRONT

Too many times we forget the sacrifices made by those who are left at home, facing the awful reality that their fathers, sons, and brothers are engaged in combat half way around the world—my mother's generation especially. They saw their husbands, brothers, and sons march off, not once, but twice in many cases. Some of them have even seen them leave three times! They deserve medals of valor, themselves. It takes a brave lady, indeed, to face that sort of stress month after month.

For instance my own dear mother, Nita Smith Garrison, had at least one of her family overseas for five years in World War II. Then she had her only two sons recalled for the Korean War, and she worried about us for all the time we were over there. All together, that is about seven years of worry, which was enough for one lady to endure.

Mom made a wonderful war wife and war mother. She frequently wrote to us all, and her letters were full of heartening things that helped us to no end. She was a teacher, and her outlook remained young until she died. Her letters were full of interesting things, and several of my buddies who had no mother to hear from looked forward to hearing from her almost as much as I did. After I read her letters, I always passed them around to my pals to read. They loved her until she was gone and kept contact with her long after they came home.

Mrs. Joseph Don Garrison, Sr. (Nita Ellen Smith), was a loving and supportive wife, mother, grandmother, and great-grandmother of Oklahoma Thunderbirds. She kept the "home fires burning" while her men were overseas.

She never forgot a service man in need of letters from home. In the last year of her life, my son-in-law, First Lieutenant Scott Collins, went to Desert Storm with his Regular Army artillery unit. Mom wrote to him once a week although she was more than 90 years old at the time and suffered from Parkinson's disease. Although her handwriting was not as perfect as it once was, she still did her best to keep Scott in good spirits. Surely there is a special place in heaven for women like her.

When we were growing up, Mom would insist that we clean our plates at every meal. She had seen some hard times, and she did not believe in waste. She would always say, "Think of all the starving little Chinese children. Clean your plates." After mom died, I was reading through letters she had saved, and there was a letter from my brother, which he had sent from Korea. He started the letter this way, "Mom, remember all those starving little Chinese children we cleaned our plates for all those years? Well, they're shooting at us now!"

She baked cookies to mail overseas weekly. We all waited for those boxes, too. The mail clerk recognized them when they arrived, and a crowd would soon show up to help me eat her delicious goodies. Mom loved for me to write and tell her about that.

Once she thought I had not been writing her enough. Shortly afterward the Chaplain's jeep showed up at our battery. Chaplain Dallas Boren, the uncle of my friend David Boren, stepped out of his jeep and marched into my command bunker. He said, "Captain Garrison, I'm surprised that you haven't been writing to your mother often enough. She has written me and asked me to talk to you about that. You had better get with it, or I'm going to give you trouble!" Dallas Boren had been a chaplain in Europe, in World War II, and we all loved his solid experience and support over in Korea. We looked forward to his frequent visits, and I certainly listened to his advice. I sat down and wrote her a letter right then, and I never failed to write at least once a week after that. I told mom about that visit, and she said, "I'll write to your colonel if it ever happens again." It never did.

Forty-fifth Division Artillery Chaplain, Captain Dallas L. Boren, brother of Lyle Boren, Congressman, and uncle of David L. Boren, former Governor of Oklahoma, United States Senator, and now President of the University of Oklahoma. Dallas L. Boren served in Europe as a Captain in the Chaplain Corps. This photograph was taken in Europe, during World War II. He served in combat in France and Germany for many months. It is said that at the time of his commission, Dallas L. Boren was the youngest Chaplain in the Corps. He was much beloved by those he served with in Korea.

Private First Class Donald P. Younce, on Multnomah County, Oregon, was a popular soldier among the men of Battery B. Unfortunately Younce was killed in action on July 10, 1952. Notice the stack of boxes on the right of the photograph. The boxes have been covered by camouflage netting to hide them from enemy observers.

A wounded American soldier is being loaded onto an evacuation helicopter at the headquarters of the Second Battalion, 180th Infantry Regiment in Korea. Helicopters were used extensively in Korea to evacuate wounded troops to field hospitals. Because the helicopters were too small to carry the wounded inside the airframe, a pod was attached to the landing skids. The wounded man was strapped into the pod, which was then closed, and carried to the nearest medical facility. The small level area in front of the headquarters was the only place the helicopter could land on the steep mountainside.

CHAPTER 29

MY BROTHER'S KEEPER

My only brother, whom I have mentioned previously, was a member of the 179th Infantry Regiment. Throughout our service in the Korean Conflict, we were never more than five miles apart. That did not mean that we saw each other often. In a combat situation it was not always easy for us to make contact with one another.

Once, in about the middle of our service in Korea, my brother's jeep came down the road and stopped near my command post. J. D., as we called him, crawled out of the jeep and climbed up to the bunker where we were. He seemed in a somber mood, and I asked him what the trouble was. He had a wife and two little sons at home, and I knew he missed them a lot. He said, "Well I won the right to purchase a new camera in the PX raffle this morning, and it costs $175. Because I have sent my money home to Ginger and the boys, I am going to have to let the camera go back to someone else. That is, unless you can lend me the money, because you are single and all." He explained that the camera was a Konica, which was highly valued by Americans.

I had been waiting months to go on "rest and recuperation" back to Tokyo. Finally my turn had come, and I was to go back for four days of R & R with all that entailed. I had saved $200 for the trip. That seemed to be what one needed for the enjoyment of an R & R.

I told J. D. that I would give him my $200 and that I would cancel my R & R at least for now. He seemed a little hesitant, but not too much, now that I think of it. He said he was most appreciative of the

On the left is the author, Captain Denzil Garrison, wearing a parka and armed with a .45-caliber pistol carried on his pistol belt. On the right is his brother, Captain Joseph Don Garrison, Jr., wearing a field jacket and armed with a .45-caliber pistol carried in a shoulder holster. Denzil Garrison served with Battery B, 171 Field Artillery in Korea and Joseph Don Garrison, Jr., served the First Battalion of the 179th Infantry Regiment in Korea. They were both Thunderbirds and proud of it. The photograph was taken on a mountainside near the frontlines in 1951.

loan, and would certainly pay me back as soon as possible. He said the camera would be worth its weight in gold in that he could send pictures home to his wife and sons, when he got his hands on that Konica. He was most effusive in his lamentations of brotherly love toward me as he pocketed my $200. He got back in his jeep and left.

I felt like a true martyr in that I had given up my leave so that my brother could get his hands on a camera to chronicle our war for his young sons. As much as I wanted to go to Tokyo, I was glad that I could make the sacrifice for my older brother. I was sure my mother and father would be proud of me for what I had done for him. I slept well that night, for I knew that I had done something fine and unselfish for my brother who had come to me for help.

The next morning, I had the urge to talk to my brother again to tell him how glad I was to have helped him get the camera, and to find out if he had purchased it yet. I called him through the regimental switchboard, reaching down to his battalion until a voice finally said, "First

Captain Joseph Don Garrison, Jr., peers through his "new Konica camera" that he took with him on leave to Tokyo, Japan. The elder Garrison borrowed the money for the camera from his younger brother and then used it to go on R & R in Japan by showing up at the airport and answering "here" when his younger brother's name was called for the flight manifest.

Battalion headquarters." I asked, "May I speak to Captain Garrison?" The operator answered, "Sorry, sir, he left this morning for R & R in Tokyo."

I found later that he did not even have to add himself to the R & R roster. My name was on the manifest, as "Captain Garrison." When they called that name, he just answered "here!" and got on the plane. His buddies told me that halfway across the Sea of Japan, they cracked a bottle, and passed it around, making toasts. My brother's toast was, "To my little brother, who is so kind and helpful to me, although he is not very smart!" I think I learned a lesson from all that, but I am damned if I know what it is. At any rate, I got what I had coming to me, when I think of all the things I had done to him while growing up. For instance, once when I was ten, I tied his big toe to the bedstead with a heavy shoelace while he slept. I then threw ice water on him. He jumped from the bed and dislocated his big toe. He swore he would get even some day, and he did!

When we both got home, my father was furious when he heard about the R & R caper. He insisted that my brother pay me back, which he did. At $20 a month it only took him 10 months to get me paid, without interest.

Oh yes, I was able to go on R & R the next month. I had a hell of a time, too.

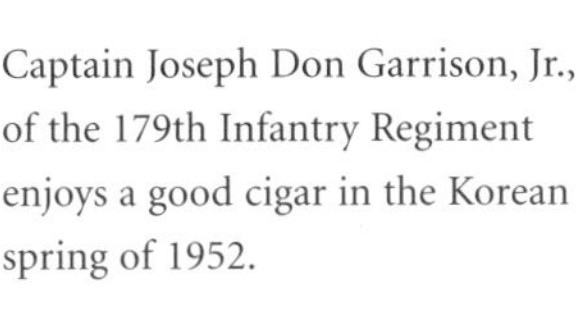

Captain Joseph Don Garrison, Jr., of the 179th Infantry Regiment enjoys a good cigar in the Korean spring of 1952.

CHAPTER 30

THINGS GET TOUGHER

As the summer of 1952 progressed, the war got tougher. This was understandable when one considered that the enemy with his primitive supply system had been in a stable line for some months. Each replacement that came up had carried one or two artillery rounds. After some months of that, the enemy stockpiled quite a supply of artillery ammunition. He was beginning to use it in ever increasing quantities that summer of 1952.

No longer could we be sure that we would not be shot at when we showed ourselves to the enemy. The enemy could shoot, too. Some people learned that the hard way.

Day by day the tempo of the war picked up. It was still basically an artillery duel and air war for us, but our infantry became more assertive and limited offensive operations were planned to give us the maximum strength for the peace talks at the little village of Panmunjam.

More than once the Americans would claim to occupy a hill, and the Chinese would dispute that claim. In that crazy war it became commonplace for those American officers at the peace table to call by field phone directly to the headquarters of units occupying the disputed real estate to ascertain who was right about the situation. Many times, both sides would plan and carry out offensive thrusts in order to master the conference table the next morning. A strange war, indeed.

But that summer fighting escalated by the day. Finally, our artillery was firing at a rate that exceeded the heaviest battles of World War II. In the last seven days I spent with my battery before I went to the battalion fire direction center, we fired the astounding total of 7,000 rounds of 105-mm. ammunition. We had to send one howitzer at a time back constantly to division ordinance to replace worn-out tubes. We would fire those pieces until the lands, built into the tubes to put a spin on the shell, came out with the projectile. They were just worn out. Eventually every light artillery piece in the division had at least one barrel replaced. This meant that we had to shoot with five weapons, instead of the normal six, while the barrel was being replaced. Ordnance did a magnificent job of replacing those tubes in a hurry, and properly, too.

When I left my battery, I was to all intents and purposes deaf in both ears. Back in those days we wore no protection for our ears, and we paid for it. In today's Army earplugs are required for members of a firing battery. In those days such things were regarded as "sissy." Very few of the old soldiers who were left with permanent hearing damage would consider ear plugs as a sissy matter now. My hearing came back partially about half way across the Pacific on the way home, but it was permanently impaired. As a lawyer, I have paid a heavy price for that

First Lieutenant Giles Crisler, who served as a forward observer, looking over the front from the observation post on Hill 324 in May of 1952. In later years Crisler became a brigadier general and maintained his contacts with his Oklahoma comrades. Crisler's weapon was the binoculars he is holding. With them he could call down immediate artillery fire on enemy targets. Note the stovepipe sticking out of the top of Crisler's observation post.

A 105-mm. howitzer crew of Battery B in the midst of a firefight. The photograph is unclear because the weapon fired at the same time the picture was taken. Three members of the howitzer's seven-man crew are shown. The other four men are preparing ammunition for firing.

This Chinese soldier, captured by the 180th Infantry Regiment, had been issued a quilted uniform to help him survive the harsh Korean winter. Once the frontline became stabilized prisoners were difficult to capture. Chinese and North Korean troops suffered tremendously during the fighting. American aerial superiority made it difficult for the enemy to keep his frontline troops adequately supplied and smoke from any fires that were started for warmth immediately drew American artillery fire. This soldier's main interest after being captured was food.

injury. I wonder how many cases I might have lost through the years, because I just did not hear something clearly in court. That answer I will never know.

One of the things about the Korean War that was so hard on our hearing was the frozen state of the landscape in those long winter months. The ground was frozen at least 18 inches deep in the winter, and the shock of artillery fire was not absorbed by the earth. The shock waves came unabated and slammed into the eardrums of us all in the firing batteries. Any old artilleryman knows what "artillery ears" means. It happened to everyone. Just a hazard of the trade, I guess. Anyway, we had it infinitely better than the infantry did.

The Chinese became much more aggressive toward the end of May in 1952, and their artillery became increasingly effective. Their patrols came closer to our lines, and even penetrated them at times. Major General David L. Ruffner was our division commander at that time, having replaced James C. Styron. It became necessary, at least to Major General Ruffner, that we strengthen our front by seizing 11 selected terrain features on our front that were either unoccupied or occupied by the enemy.

In a very successful operation these objectives were quickly won between 4 to 7 June 1952. Ten of the objectives were secured, the one remaining being the aptly named "Point Eerie," which will never be forgotten by any soldier who ever saw it sticking up, as I said before, like a great pimple out in no-man's land. Finally, Eerie was taken, and "Pokkae Ridge,' the 12th objective, was seized. Our lines were the most secure they had ever been.

The enemy reacted in a most violent manner. He hit with everything he had, including furious artillery barrages. Old Baldy and Pork Chop became the targets for heavy enemy attacks. We fired artillery in their support continually. Our cannoneers were worn out, but the infantry said we saved the day out on the front. We took great pride in that.

The division was finally relieved after almost 10 months on the front. The Second, or Indian Head, Division took over our sector, and the 45th Division pulled back to rest and lick its wounds. The first night after we left the line huge waves of Chinese were thrown at what had been our sector. They almost succeeded in penetrating the front, and we were quickly put into a blocking position backing up the Second and Seventh Divisions, which were taking heavy losses.

When we were pulled out of the line many of the Thunderbirds, who had been there longest, including myself, began the trip back home to Uncle Sugar. The heavy fighting resulted in a slowdown of our rotation, and we were betting that we would be sent up again to stop the Chinese. We held our breath, and we breathed a little easier when we neared the Port of Inchon, where our troopship was waiting. Once we were on the way home, alive, it did not seem fair that they would change their minds and send us back to the front.

Finally, we reached Inchon, still holding our breath. I was in the shipment with several hundred enlisted men, and also with Colonel Frederick A. Daugherty, who had been the commander of the 179th

Infantry Regiment. He was a remarkable leader with the gaze of an eagle. I always thought that no man could look into those piercing eyes, and tell anything but the truth. He later became a federal judge, where he served very credibly, and later still commanded the division when it reverted to National Guard status. He was a fine soldier, and he looked every inch the part.

We found that we were to travel to Japan on a Victory ship, the SS *Sadao Munemori.* It was named for a Nisei Japanese who won the Medal of Honor in World War II. It was not an imposing ship, but we loved it because it was going to take us on the first leg of the trip home.

When we arrived at Inchon, a large barge awaited us. About 400 officers and men crowded on it, and the barge was moved into the Yellow Sea taking us to where the ship was anchored far out in the water. The tide at Inchon is one of the highest in the world, and shipping can come into the docks only at special times. The tide was out, and we were taken several miles out in the bay to the *Sadao Munemori.* When we pulled up to the ship, we saw that there was no gangplank for boarding. Over the sides of the ship were dangling scramble nets, which we knew we would have to climb if we were to get on the ship. We certainly intended to get aboard, for sure.

A scramble net is just a very loose woven net made of strong rope about an inch in diameter which troops use to climb on and off of troopships. Anyone who knows about amphibious landings knows what an ordeal it is to climb up or down one of those nets, especially while carrying all our baggage as we were. It was no easy feat.

Colonel Daugherty and I were the first to start the climb. All the GIs waiting their turn began to rawhide us with wisecracks and catcalls as we tried to make that treacherous climb. They were protected by anonymity because they were from various units, unknown even to each other. American soldiers are not at their best in that sort of a situation. They sometimes turn into "wise guys" when they would not think of doing and saying such things back in their outfits.

Colonel Daugherty started up the net carrying a huge barracks bag over one shoulder, and a large B-4 bag containing all his uniforms in one hand. All in all, he must have been carrying well over 150 pounds of equipment and clothing. That only left him one hand to use in the climb up to the deck of the ship.

I was right behind him, carrying a brief case and a large barracks bag. I was loaded down pretty well myself. I looked up and saw that B-4 bag swinging ominously as he climbed, and I saw that he was carrying about all he could. I climbed a little faster, and finally reached him. I put my shoulder under that B-4 bag, and we climbed the rest of the way together. Colonel Daugherty and I have been fast friends ever since that long climb to start on our way home.

All the way up the net the GIs on the barge hooted and derided us. We just took it in our stride knowing there was not really anything we could do about it. We made it to the deck, and then had the privilege of turning around and watching our tormentors climbing the same net. Several of them fell off into the water, and we took some solace in that. To this day, I do not know why the Navy did not have some sort of a gangplank rigged up so we would not have to make such a climb under those trying circumstances. But we were on the way home, and shortly the Sadao Munemori turned out into the Yellow Sea and started on the three-day trip to Sasebo, Japan. The Korean War was behind us.

Colonel Frederick A. Daugherty commanded the 179th Infantry Regiment in Korea. During World War II he served in the Pacific Theater on the staff of General Walter Krueger. Daughtery later rose to the rank of major general and commanded the 45th Infantry Division. He was a superb infantry leader. After Korea he became a United States District Judge for the Western District of Oklahoma.

CHAPTER 31

BACK TO THE LAND OF THE RISING SUN

When the *Sadao Munemori* reached Sasebo, Japan, we knew that the chances were that we were going to make it on home. Still, the gnawing worry persisted that we might be called back because the situation up on the front had become very tense. We read about the terrific fight on Old Baldy and Pork Chop Hill, and we completely understood what our replacements were facing. But the call to return to Korea never came.

Sasebo was the largest American naval base in the Japanese Islands. It was not hard to envision what it must have been like during World War II, when Admiral Isoruku Yamamato and his cohorts held sway. The Japanese are a capable race, and they became Americanized to an astounding degree during our occupation. Certainly more so than the Germans, whom I came to know well in the Army of Occupation over in Europe. We really had not the slightest uneasiness in being out alone at any hour in that seaport city on Kyushu, one of the main Japanese home islands.

There was a club for Americans there called Matsu Lodge atop the highest hill in Sasebo. The story was that it was the favorite hangout for Japanese Naval Officers during World War II. I do not know if that was true, but I know that every junior officer in the American Army who came through Sasebo on the way home from Korea, made it up to the Matsu Lodge at least once during his stay in port. Usually a soldier would have to wait from a week to 10 days for a troopship home.

That would give each person several visits to Matsu while in Sasebo. Most any junior officer you find who came home through Sasebo will either admit he had been there with a wry smile, or he will lie and tell you he never heard of the place. We all went there, at least those of us who were single.

I was assigned a berth on the USS *General Pope,* a large troopship that was a sister ship of the vessel on which I had come from the United States to Japan. We waited several days before the ship was ready to be loaded.

Two of my closest friends, First Lieutenant Bill Sumter and First Lieutenant Bud Eddleman, were due in Sasebo two days after I arrived. They had both been my buddies even back in college. I went down to the dock to watch for their ship so I could greet them. I checked with the military transportation officer there in Sasebo and found that they were aboard a ship which he named, and where it was to dock. They were about as close to me as anyone, and they were both in my wedding when I was married after the Korean War.

The large ship docked, and I looked on deck to see if my friends were there. I heard a far away voice say, "Garrison!" Finally I spotted my buddies away up on the top deck of that ship, which was much larger than the one which brought me to Japan from Korea. They waved, and Sumter, who was a joker of the highest order, yelled down to me, "Eddleman fell in the crapper!" Eddleman pushed him to shut him up and all the people on the ship and on the dock got a kick out of what Sumter had said.

When they made it ashore the full story came out. It seems that while they were in Yongdongpo at the staging area in Korea for the trip home, they had gone to a tent that was made into an officer's club for the use of the casual officers who passed through there on the way home.

It seems that there was a large open sewer, which was not at all strange in Korea, between their tent and the tent where the officer's club was set up. Also, it seems that there was not a bridge over the sewer, but only a two by ten board across the thing, which was about four feet deep with sewage.

They made it over the board all right on the way over. But coming back Sumter saw that Eddleman was in no shape to navigate over the board, and offered to help him across. Eddleman "Get your hands off of me, I'll walk across on my own." Sumter shrugged and told him to go ahead. Sumter made it over, but Eddleman fell into the sewer up to his chest. He tried to crawl out the steep sides, but he would slip back into the raw sewage that made the sides of the trench very slippery. He asked Sumter to take him by the hand and pull him out, and he held a very slimy hand up to him. Sumter said, "I'm not going to touch that hand. You fell in by yourself, now get out by yourself!" He went back to their tent and told his tent mates what had transpired.

After several more tries, Eddleman finally made it out of that stinking open sewer. When he got back to the tent, considerably sobered up, he was met by all the other occupants, who made him strip right then and go to the shower tent before he could come into their tent. They then made him throw away his ruined uniform, which he did without argument. Eddleman found that his best friend, Sumter, would do most anything for him, except help him out of an open Korean sewer.

They are both gone now, and I miss them. We remained the best of friends throughout their lives. In their own way, they were excellent soldiers.

CHAPTER 32

A MATTER OF CONSCIENCE

The seaport of Sasebo had a distinct Oklahoma flavor in August of 1952. The last of the guardsmen were on our way home, and a very relieved group we were. We pinched ourselves to make sure we were not dreaming. All of us believed we were fortunate, indeed. There must have been the better part of a thousand Oklahomans in Sasebo awaiting a berth on a troopship home.

One of those returnees was my good friend Joe Hendrix, who came from Weleetka, Oklahoma. Joe had been reared by a courageous widowed mother, who lived in a very small and unpretentious wooden frame house in that little town. A schoolteacher, she inculcated a love of learning and a search for knowledge in her son. Although he and I did not agree on many things politically, we were nonetheless close friends.

Joe came to me in the bachelor officers quarters at the port of debarkation, and said he had arranged a really good deal for me. Joe, student that he was, spoke pretty fluent Japanese by this time. He had met a Japanese girl there in Sasebo who was anxious to find a young American officer to meet her sister, who was just now coming from a rural prefecture into the wild goings on of Sasebo. Joe explained that the older "Musame," which meant girl, wanted her younger sister to become the concubine of a young American captain, or Tai-san, as the Japanese described my rank.

The older sister said that her little sister was entirely innocent, and as a matter of fact, was a virgin. Japan is a militaristic nation, with generations of warriors in her background, and the older sister wanted to pick out just the right American officer for her younger sister who was newly arrived from unsophisticated rural Japan. She, for some reason, told Joe that I just fit the bill. As a 26-year-old captain, who had spent nearly five years in the American Army, I was not all that much experienced myself. But I thought I was.

On the appointed night I was told to meet Joe and the older girl at a club in Sasebo. I dressed up in a clean uniform with all my ribbons attached, and went to town. There, I met this charming little creature who immediately reminded me of "Liat," in the play South Pacific. She was innocent, and beautiful. Her shyness was pronounced, and it was most becoming. When she spoke to me she diverted her gaze to the floor, and looked up only occasionally. She wore a colorful Kimono, which could not completely hide the thin and lithe young oriental body it covered. I was captivated. She seemed to be, too, in her shy way.

Soon Joe suggested that we all go to the house of his girl, the older sister. After a short walk we arrived at the little paper house built in the classic Japanese style and sat around a table without our shoes and drank sake. The younger girl, who was known as Michiko, soon became rosy-cheeked from the wine, and a little intoxicated.

Presently Joe and his girl excused themselves and left the room. I took Michiko by the hand and led her into the little Japanese bedroom that had been set aside for us, equipped with the traditional Japanese bed, spread out on the floor. Quietly and quickly Michiko slipped out of her clothes and into the bed. I removed my uniform and did the same.

I shall never forget the concern that showed on her face, nor will I ever forget her innocent charm. I was spellbound. After a caress, I realized that this little beauty had never even been kissed before. Obviously, she was just as her sister had described her, a complete virgin. I looked at her slim body trembling from fear and expectation. I began to have second thoughts myself. Was this an honorable and proper thing I was preparing to do? I thought not.

Reluctantly, I began to put my uniform back on. I tried to tell her in my halting Japanese, that I just could not be the one to take her virginity. Although she knew very little English, I think she understood. She smiled meekly and squeezed my hand. Knowing that she was very poor by our standards, I slipped a thousand-yen note into her hand and carried my shoes out into the vestibule of the little house, as was the custom. I put on those shoes and walked back to my quarters feeling somehow very clean and proud of myself. I never saw Michiko again.

I was sure that there would be another young American officer in that bedroom in short order, probably the next night. I also knew that he would not be as conscience-stricken as I. I have always been glad and proud that I had not ended her childhood in that little Japanese bedroom. That would be on somebody else's conscience, if he had one.

Joe said the next day that he thought I was crazy, but he understood, I think. He died during an emergency surgery, less than six weeks after we got home.

CHAPTER 33

SETTING THE RECORD STRAIGHT

Some years ago, a certain businessman was in my office, and the subject of conversation turned to the Korean War. This particular person had been a sailor in World War II, and had gotten a commission from attending Reserve Officer Training Corps (ROTC) training after the war. He had been called up when the Korean War started, and he was sent over there, where he became a member of the First Cavalry Division. He was full of stories of valor, mostly including himself as the main actor. Finally, he asked me, "And what outfit did you belong to?" I told him I had been in the 45th Division.

He snorted and said, "The war was over before you occupation troops ever got there."

I told him in no uncertain terms that the First Cavalry Division was in a sorry state when I saw them, and I got angrier as I continued. He left, and I thought of my comrades who never made it home and how unfair his remarks had been to their memory. I made up my mind to search the records to prove the fallacies of his statements. That promise I made to myself was in the back of my mind for many years, and at last I have come to the point of answering his foolish and unsubstantiated remarks.

To start with, there was enough blood and sacrifice to go around to every soldier who served in that war, regardless of when he served. I submit that a soldier killed in 1951, 1952, or 1953 was just as dead as one shot in 1950. That braggart had insulted the service of all those

Lieutenant Colonel William E. Murphy the commander of the First Battalion, 179th Infantry Regiment in Korea. Colonel Murphy was an excellent infantry commander, who served with the 45th Division in Italy, France, and Germany in World War II. His experience and leadership made him one of the best infantry battalion commanders in Korea. Note the suntan line on Murphy's forehead caused by the constant wearing of a steel helmet. In the upper right is the side of his sandbagged command post.

Sergeant First Class Floyd K. Clark, of McAlester, Oklahoma, is seated on the right. On the left is Private First Class Orlind S. Case of Albany, Georgia. Clark was Battery B's supply sergeant and Case was his helper. The two men are seated around one of the stoves used to heat tents in the winter. Note the sand filled container in which the stove is placed to keep it from overheating the tent's wooden floor.

brave men and their sacrifices that served after him. I have done extensive research on the war since that time, and especially on the 45th Division and its service and losses in Korea. As I stated before, more men were killed after we started the peace talkes with the Communists, than were suffered before we went to the peace table. With that in mind, I have researched the losses of the 45th Thunderbirds in Korea. We need not bow to the record of any other unit there. We gave our share to the freedom of South Korea.

During its time in Korea, the 45th Infantry Division suffered 4,038 casualties. That was roughly the equivalent of a full regiment. Those casualties included 834 Killed in action, 3,170 wounded in action, 1 missing in action, and 33 prisoners of war. The sacrifices that were made by Thunderbird soldiers forever marked the history of that war with valor and devotion. We need not be ashamed of our service. That businessman who disparaged our record has now become bankrupt, and moved on to places unknown. If I ever see him again, I promise that I will have a few more words for him.

The infantry regiments of the division suffered the heaviest percentage of casualties. The breakdown of the soldiers killed in action by regiment is as follows: 179th Infantry Regiment 323; 180th Infantry Regiment 301; and 279th Infantry Regiment 175. This book is dedicated to the memory of those heroes, and the others that died wearing the Thunderbird patch in that war which has become known as "The Forgotten War." In the minds and memories of those "old soldiers" still alive, their valor and sacrifice will never be forgotten. We will always remember. God Bless America!

CHAPTER 34

THE BUG OUT BOOGIE

Before we arrived in Korea, considerable fighting had all ready taken place. The Americans had retreated down the length of Korea to Pusan, where they set up the last-ditch Pusan Perimeter. They held the North Koreans there and struck back north after MacArthur invaded at Inchon in one of the most successful military moves in modern history. The North Korean lines around the Pusan Perimeter just evaporated. To a large extent, the North Korean Army disintegrated. They never really recovered from that disaster.

When the Chinese came in American units were isolated and cut to ribbons at times. The result was another withdrawal southward. This started the attitude of "The Bug Out." I was told that some American units just fired a few rounds and started south.

There was a song sung by Hank Williams that was popular in those days. It was named "Movin' On." All the GIs knew this song, and it was one of their favorites. Soon, they adapted it to their own words. They called it "The Bug Out Boogie." It went something like this:

Chinese comin' through the pass
And the UN Army's a haulin' ass
We're movin' on,

We'll soon be gone,
Gotta go, gotta blow,

Gotta Pusan go, we're movin' on.
Hear the bugles sound so shrill
If the mortars don't get you then the burp guns will,
We're movin' on,

We'll soon be gone,
Gotta go, gotta blow,
Gotta Pusan go, we're movin' on.

That darn song was being sung by the entire Army. When General Ridgway heard a GI sing that tune, he was infuriated. He put out the order that anyone caught singing Bug Out Boogie would be tried by court-martial. As you may guess, by the time we left there it was still being heard all along the front-line. Most every one over there learned the words to that song, and none of us ever "bugged out," because of it!

CHAPTER 35

KOREAN MILITARY JUSTICE

Our South Korean allies were hardy. The Koreans had been subjugated by the Chinese for centuries, and they had been occupied by the brutal Japanese for 55 years before they were freed after World War II. All in all, they are a commendable race when one considers their history.

We were assigned a group of Korean laborers, who were a part of an organization called the Korean Service Corps (KSC). They were members of a semi-military organization assigned to each unit. They were members of the South Korean Army who were assigned to the KSC and were paid to give service to the allied armies by acting as bearers and workers for the units in the line. They were not always the cleanest or most photogenic of people, but they did a lot toward keeping us supplied in those precipitous mountains, which were foreign to most of us. In retrospect, they were indispensable to us.

These laborers were called "Choggies" by the Gis. They even made a verb out of the word. "To Choggie" something up the mountain meant to carry it up on your back. As you can guess, the average GI deferred those tasks to the Choggies, when possible.

Those Choggies used a hand made A-frame backpack to carry unbelievable amounts of material and supplies up those mountains. And I say mountains, to distinguish them from hills. They were more than hills, by a long shot. The A-frames fit on the back of the Choggie, and he piled more and more items on the frame, until the weight car-

Cooks serving a hot meal to an infantry platoon on the frontline in Korea. It was amazing that so many hot meals were available under such trying circumstances. Hot meals brought higher morale. As every commander knows, an army travels on its stomach. Note the Korean Service Corps trooper on the left. They were used to carry the hot meals up the steep Korean mountainside to the Americans and were subject to the severe military justice of the South Korean Army.

ried many times outweighed the bearer himself. A GI just would not do that, if there were any way to avoid it. The Choggie was the way.

Most of them were happy to be assigned to an American unit, where the food was better, and the autocratic leadership of the South Korean Army was not so stringent. They were, however subject to discipline when the occasion called for it.

One particular time, an American soldier in my unit missed his camera. A Choggie had been seen around his hootchee, and the American went to the Korean officer in charge and told him of his suspicions. The Korean officer called all the KSC people together, and asked them about the camera. None of them admitted to the theft of it.

The officer then proceeded to search the dugout where the Choggies lived. There, he found the camera among the belongings of one particular man. He then confronted the unlucky KSC with the proof, and he confessed that he had, indeed, stolen the camera.

The Korean officer called all the KSC personnel into a central area in the battery and spoke to them in Korean. Then he armed all of them except the miscreant, with the end of a cot made of heavy hardwood. Thus armed, they formed a circle. At the command of the officer, they proceeded to beat the poor fellow senseless, breaking bones in his upraised arms in the process.

A view of the Korean frontlines in the Battery B area. Note the barbed wire entanglements and the bunkers dug into the hillside. The dugouts were made by excavating holes in the hillsides, roofing the holes with timbers, and then piling sandbags on top of the timbers. Duty on the frontlines in Korea was harsh and the living conditions were primitive.

At length, they stopped the brutal punishment just in time. Wooden casts were placed on the arms of the poor Choggie, and he was washed up to remove the blood from his head and face. The laborers then went about their tasks as though nothing had happened.

We were stunned by what we had seen. The fellow whose camera had been stolen was exceptionally upset by what his complaint had brought about. I questioned the Korean officer about what would then happen. Specifically, I asked him if there would be a court-martial for the thief. He answered, "This is our form of court-martial. We have no formal code of conduct for our troops. Each commander metes out his own form of punishment. I don't think we will have any more trouble with Koreans stealing from Americans in this battery." And, to be sure, we did not!

CHAPTER 36

AN UNLIKELY CONNECTION

There were a lot of Native Americans in the 45th Division, in both World War II and Korea. Two of them, Jack C. Montgomery, a Cherokee, and Ernest Childers, a Creek, earned the Medal of Honor in Europe during World War II. By and large, the American Indian soldier was a true warrior. I never knew one to turn and run from a battle.

As it is well known, sometimes the Indian can run afoul of liquor just like his white or black counterparts. John Barleycorn, as whiskey was called, can get the best of any man. Such was the case with a private I will call William Mangan, although that is not his real name. Mangan, a full blood Potawatomi, had enlisted in the division when we were called up in 1950. He was assigned as the driver of Brigadier General Muldrow and had no trouble until we arrived at Camp Polk.

One Sunday afternoon at Polk there was a line of soldiers out in front of the Post Theater waiting for the start of the movie. Up drove the general's car, with stars blazing from its bumpers, and screeched to a halt before all the soldiers. Someone called out, "Attention," and the line of soldiers snapped to attention. An unsteady Mangan stepped from the sedan, and opened the back door. All the soldiers expected the general to alight from the vehicle, but to the surprise and consternation of all the onlookers, a very skinny and drunk private alighted climbed out, and promptly proceeded to pass out there in front of the line of soldiers waiting to enter the theater.

The MPs were called, and Mangan and his passenger were arrested and placed in the guardhouse. That was the last of driving for Mangan. He was immediately replaced by another more sober soldier. Mangan was court-martialed by a summary court, and punished by a fine and a short period of incarceration.

I never heard any more from Mangan until I received a call from the battalion adjutant in Korea. He explained that Mangan was again in trouble for drunkenness and that he had requested to be transferred to our battery. His commanding officer had agreed to the transfer, and Mangan was on the way down to our outfit. I told the adjutant that I would give him only one chance, and if he caused any trouble, I would send him back to his original unit immediately. The adjutant agreed to that arrangement.

In a short while a jeep arrived carrying Mangan and his barracks bag. He was drunk, and he immediately picked a fight with the first sergeant, which was a very dumb thing to do and not hard to do, either. The first sergeant put him right back into the jeep, and quickly called for me. I ordered him to be taken back to his earlier unit, and reported to the adjutant what had happened. I never heard from or laid eyes on Mangan in Korea after that day.

Some months after I got home to Oklahoma, I was asleep at my parent's home in Norman on a Sunday morning. My mother knocked on the bedroom door, and informed me that an old Army buddy was there to see me. She described him, and I thought it must be Mangan. He could have been described several ways, but "old Army buddy" was not one of them. More accurately, he was in the same drunken condition he had been in when I had last seen him in Korea. I knew I was in for it.

I stepped to the door, and Mangan sneered, "Well captain, how does it feel not to have those captain's bars on to order me around?" I said, "Mangan, there are very few places where I can order you around, but you happen to be standing on one of them right now. Get the hell off my property!" I knew that trouble was going to develop, but to my surprise Mangan began to cry. He blubbered that I was the only friend he had in the world, and how sorry he was for the problems he had caused me since he had known me.

Mangan went on to say that when he came back to his Potawatomi home, he found his wife living with another man. He said this was devastating to him, and he wanted me to file a divorce for him. I explained to him that I was just then preparing to finish my last year in law school, and I would have to refer him to a lawyer who could help him. He asked me to do that.

I knew Hez Bussey, a Cherokee lawyer who had been a prisoner of the Japanese in World War II. He was a favorite of mine, who later became a justice on the Oklahoma Court of Criminal Appeals, a position he held for many years. I knew he was brand new in practice, and might appreciate a client.

I called Hez, and asked him if he could help Mangan. I told him Mangan had $75 he could give him as a retainer fee, and we agreed that Mangan would be at his office that afternoon at 2:00 p.m. Mangan left, still filled with booze.

At two in the afternoon Mangan was waiting when Hez got to his office. Mangan gave him the retainer, and began to tell his sad story of coming home from the war and finding his wife living with another man. He wailed a bit, and stated he just wanted to be rid of her even though he was broken-hearted.

Hez told him he would prepare the papers, which would be ready by noon on Monday. As he finished with talking about the legal matters, Hez asked Mangan, "What tribe do you belong to?" Mangan replied, "Potawatomi." Hez said, "You know, I was in prison camp with a Potawatomi, who was one of the best friends I ever had." Mangan asked, "Who was he?" Hez replied, "Leonard Turtle [not his real name], do you know him?" Mangan cried, "That's the son-of-a-bitch I found living with my wife when I got home!" Mangan stomped out of the office, and never returned, even to claim his retainer fee. Whether or not he ever got a divorce I don't know, but neither Hez Bussey or I ever saw him again.

CHAPTER 37

BACK TO UNCLE SUGAR

The trip home was uneventful. We were all tired to the bone, and most of the time was spent sleeping. We attended meals only enough to stay alive, and it was not all that palatable anyway. We believed we had earned a rest.

The Gateway to Home sign above the entrance to the replacement depot at Inchon, Korea, meant just what it said to members of Battery B who had completed their tour of duty in Korea. Nonetheless, as the author recalled "We held our breath until we were afloat" on ships bound for the United States. The reason was that combat operations had increased "When we left, and we half-way expected to be sent back up." Fortunately that did not happen.

The USNS *General John Pope* (AP-110) which carried the author and many other Thunderbirds back to America after their service in Korea. Named for Mexican War and Civil War Major General John Pope, the ship carried troops throughout the Pacific during both World War II and the Korean War.

The infantry soldiers were exceptionally worn out. After a year of combat, they were tired through and through. Some of them stayed in their bunks for days. For instance, my friend Paul Reed lived through that voyage while eating nothing but chocolate candy bars for sustenance. His wristwatch was a self-winding one that was activated by the movements of his arm. Back in those days, we had nothing like the little clock batteries that energize our watches now. Reed was so immobile during that trip home that his self-winding watch ran down! He went for days at a time sleeping around the clock.

After a voyage of about 10 days, as I remember, the USNS *General Pope,* which was our magic carpet home, neared the Golden Gate

Bridge in San Francisco. Looking at that marvelous structure, I thought of the last time I had seen it, over a year before. I had wondered before if I would ever see it again, and here it was. The 5,000 troops on that ship were quietly watching the approaching tugs, and most of them were thanking their maker for this day. There were not all that many dry eyes aboard.

As we neared the dock, we heard an angel's voice from a loud speaker. A lovely redhead was singing Oscar Straus' beautiful song, "My Hero." We all thought that she was singing to each of us, individually. I never found out her name, but I love her to this very day. I hope the ensuing years treated her well.

We picked up our bags, and shuffled ashore. When I got on the grass near the dock, I kneeled down and kissed the soil of Uncle Sugar. How sweet it was!

The USNS *General John Pope.*

CHAPTER 38

THE THUNDERBIRD TRADITION

Citizen soldiering has been a serious subject in my family for generations. Three of my four great-grandfathers and one great, great grandfather had been Union soldiers in the Civil War, and one of them was left for dead on the battlefield at Franklin, Tennessee. Happily, he did not die, and he escaped from his Confederate captors in a most exciting way, and lived another 60 years after the war.

Then there were my father, Joseph Don Garrison, Sr., and my uncle Homer Ralph Garrison, who served in World War I with the Oklahoma National Guard. They went to combat in France with the 36th Infantry Division, with which the National Guard troops from Oklahoma served in that war. When my father and his brother went down to sign up, my grandfather went with them. He asked the recruiting officer if he had a place for him. The officer told him, "We would have only a non-combatant job for a man your age." Grandfather asked, "What does that mean?" The officer answered, "That means that you wouldn't be carrying a gun." Grandfather chewed on his tobacco and pondered on that a minute, and remarked, "I don't want to get over there without a gun!" So Grandfather watched his two sons march off from Cherokee, Oklahoma, down a path which eventually led them to the Meuse-Argonne in France.

My favorite tale about my father's service was the story he told me about one of his men with the incredible name of Penos Parker. Over in the Meuse-Argonne, my father was an 18 year old corporal manning a machine gun out on the front, with Parker. In the middle of the night Parker said to my father, "Corporal, I know everybody in the company thinks I am just an eight-ball. Well, they would be too if they had happen to them what happened to me." My father asked, "What was that, Penos?" Parker went on, "I worked on a cable tool drilling rig in the oil field, and I was on duty in the middle of the night. The rig broke down, and we were told to go home. I walked seven miles home, and went in my house and found my best friend in bed with my wife." My father gasped and asked, "Did you kill him?" Penos Parker answered, "No, but I never cared for that son of a bitch after that!"

My father organized Company D of the 179th Infantry Regiment of the 45th Infantry Division in 1925. He commanded that company for years. When the division was called up in 1940, my father was a major and soon he was a lieutenant colonel. He became the commander of the Second Battalion of the 180th Infantry. This was a cracker-jack outfit that produced three Medal of Honor winners before the war was over.

My father's heart was broken when he was ordered overseas more than a year before the division left for Europe and was assigned to staff duty in England. He never recovered his spark after that disappointment, and he carried the hurt to his grave. He was sent home ill from England, and he never really recovered for the rest of his life.

But my father instilled love of the military in a lot of people in his time. Not the least of these was my uncle, William Carl Garrison, who had enlisted in my father's company as a buck private. By the time the division was called up, he had become an officer after attending the University of Oklahoma. He entered World War II service with the division in 1940, as an artillery officer. He went to the advanced officer's course at Fort Sill and graduated first in his class. They kept him at Fort Sill as a gunnery instructor, and later gave him command of the first eight-inch howitzer battalion in the American Army. He trained that unit and took it to Normandy. His battalion, the 738th Field Artillery Battalion, became famous through its exploits with the eight-inch howitzers. Among us artillerymen that is the greatest artillery piece ever made.

Uncle Bill, as we called him in the family, came home a full colonel. He loved the Army, and stayed in as a Regular Army officer after the war. He was finally promoted to major general, and served in his last assignment for three years as the Inspector General of the United States Army. That was a matter of much pride to us in the family, as we all knew that Major General Friedrich Wilhelm Augustus von Steuben himself had been the first Inspector General.

My brother, Joseph Don Garrison, Jr., and I had both attended officer's candidate school in World War II, and we both served in Europe. My brother entered the Korean War service as a captain of infantry, and I came in as a first lieutenant of field artillery. He served in the 179th Infantry Regiment, and I served in the 171st Field Artillery Battalion.

Another Garrison who served in the division was a cousin of ours, First Lieutenant Frank L. Garrison, who served in Company F of the 179th Infantry Regiment. He made a real name for himself as an infantry combat leader, and was highly decorated. He was severely wounded on 5 July 1952. Frank was one of those men destined to be an infantryman. His men respected him and his superiors depended on him. He remained in the Regular Army after Korea, and did three tours in Vietnam. He was finally promoted to be the G-3, in charge operations and plans of the famous 101st Airborne Division, of Battle of Bastogne fame, where he made a fine record for himself and the family. He was a full colonel when he left the Army. He would make a fine subject for a book. We are proud to call him one of ours.

My father drove me back down to Camp Polk after my last leave home before shipping out for the Far East. He was very quiet as we drove south, and I knew he was thinking deeply. When we arrived and it came time to say goodbye, my father gripped the steering wheel as I stood at the car window. He never was much to show emotion, and he told me to watch myself over there. He made me promise to do that, and he haltingly told me how proud he was of his two sons. He just sat there looking away for a long time, and he finally looked directly at me and I could see that he was crying for the second time since I had known him. The first time was at the funeral of his mother. I hugged him, and he backed the car out of the parking lot. I waved goodbye to him. I did not see him again for almost two years.

The Thunderbird tradition has been handed down to those now serving in my family and was duplicated by thousands of other families that tied to the Thunderbird mystique. My son, Charles A. Garrison, who started as a private in the 179th Infantry, became a lieutenant colonel in the Regular Army. He was a Ranger and a Paratrooper. I am very proud of him. He was respected by those he served under, and those who serve under him. My son-in-law, Scott E. Collins, is now a major in the 45th. He graduated from the United States Military Academy at West Point, after entering the service as a private in the 179th Infantry. He served in an artillery unit in Desert Storm and was a part of the famous "Hail Mary" thrust to the Euphrates River described by General Norman Schwarzkopf in his famous critique. Then there is Major James C. Flowers, also my son-in-law, who serves as United States Military Attache to the Kingdom of Morocco. He is an officer in military intelligence. I am proud of them all, and they are living up to the heritage set in motion by my father and his family. Four generations of our family have served, now that my grandson, Reid Isaac Garrison has enlisted as a private in the 180th Infantry. His younger brother, Cole Gordon Garrison also is a private in the 180th now. I am sure that some of my other six grandsons will follow the flag. That is expected of them.

Oklahomans make good soldiers. This is recognized throughout the Army. The Thunderbirds of today are making their name as important parts of our national defense. Although we all pray they will never again be called upon to serve in combat situations, if the occasion ever arises, they will not be found wanting. God bless the USA!

As a young man, Joseph Don Garrison of Cherokee Oklahoma, joined the Oklahoma National Guard and served in World War I with the 36th Infantry Division as an infantry machine gunner. He earned two battle stars in that war. After graduating from college he moved to Norman, Oklahoma, and helped organize Company D, 179th Infantry Regiment, of the Oklahoma National Guard in 1925. Garrison was mobilized in 1940 as a major and was quickly promoted to lieutenant colonel. He served in England during World War II and commanded the Second Battalion of the 180th Infantry for 18 months prior to going overseas.
The elder Garrison retired from reserve status as a colonel and built a good foundation for all the Garrisons who followed him in the Oklahoma National Guard. He is the father of the author.

William Carl Garrison, first entered the Oklahoma National Guard in 1928 when he joined the 45th Infantry Division at Cherokee, Oklahoma. He attended the University of Oklahoma and received a degree in engineering. William Garrison became an artillery officer in the 45th Division in 1936 and was called to active duty in 1940 as a captain in the field artillery. William Garrison attended the officers advanced course at Fort Sill, Oklahoma, in 1941, and graduated first in his class. He remained at Fort Sill as an instructor in the Gunnery Department until he was given command of the first 8-inch howitzer battalion in the United States Army.
As a lieutenant colonel, he took his battalion to Europe and landed at the Normandy beachhead. His battalion, the 738th, fought across Europe into Czechoslovakia. At the end of World War II he had risen to the rank of colonel. William Garrison remained in the Regular Army, was promoted first to brigadier general and then to major general. He eventually became Inspector General of the United States Army before retiring He is the uncle of the author.

Joseph Don Garrison, Jr., entered the service with the 45th Infantry Division in 1940. He became a sergeant in the 180th Infantry, and left Camp Barkley, Texas, to attend officer candidate school at Fort Benning, Georgia, and graduated in 1941 as a second lieutenant of infantry. He went to Europe with the 94th Infantry Division, and fought in several campaigns. He returned to the United States after the war as a captain. He was well decorated in Europe. After graduation from the University of Oklahoma with a geology degree, he again became a member of the 45th Infantry Division. Joseph Don Garrison, Jr., was called to active duty with the 45th Division in 1950 and went to Japan and Korea as a member of the First Battalion, 179th Infantry Regiment. After he returned to civilian life, he became a lieutenant colonel in the reorganized 45th Division, and served as a battalion commander. He retired as a lieutenant colonel. He is the brother of the author.

Denzil D. Garrison, entered the United States Army in 1945 and attended basic training and officer candidate school at Fort Sill, Oklahoma. He graduated as a second lieutenant of field artillery and was sent to Europe where he served with the Ninth Infantry Division Artillery and the 71st Constabulary Squadron. He returned to the United States after his service and entered the University of Oklahoma's School of Law. Denzil Garrison was called to active duty during his senior year of law school for service in Korea as a first lieutenant of the 45th Division Artillery. Immediately upon mobilization he was assigned as battery executive officer of Battery B, 171st First Artillery Battalion. He became the battery commander in Japan, and took the battery to Korea, where it served as direct support of the 180th Infantry Regiment.
He was promoted to captain in Korea and returned to the United States in the fall of 1952. He served in the United States Army Reserve after graduating from the University of Oklahoma School of Law and reached the rank of major.

Frank L. Garrison entered the service as a first lieutenant of infantry with the 45th Infantry Division when it was mobilized in 1950. He was a resident of Lawton, Oklahoma. He commanded Company F, 179th Infantry Regiment in Japan and Korea. He lead a patrol to Pokkae Ridge in May of 1952, and performed with valor, winning decorations for his actions in a two-hour firefight in which he was gravely wounded. Frank Garrison returned to the United States as a captain after his tour in Korea and entered the Regular Army where he served with distinction. He served three tours in Vietnam and became a general staff member, G-3 in charge of operations and plans, of the 101st Airborne Division. He received many decorations for his service, including several purple hearts. He retired as a colonel of infantry. He is a cousin of the author Denzil D. Garrison.

Charles Alfred Garrison began his military career in 1975 when he enlisted in Company C, 179th Infantry Regiment as a private. He attended basic training and advanced infantry training at Fort Benning, Georgia. In 1976, he was admitted to officer candidate school at Fort Benning, and graduated on March 3, 1977, as a second lieutenant of infantry. He entered active duty with the United States Army after graduation from Southwestern Oklahoma State University at Weatherford, Oklahoma, in 1980. His first assignment was at Fort Benning as a first lieutenant training officer. He was promoted to captain during that assignment.
Charles Garrison was assigned to the 25th Infantry Division in Hawaii for three years and was promoted to major. He was then assigned to the Joint Readiness Training Center in Little Rock, Arkansas, with a field expertise of light infantry. His next assignment was at the Headquarters, United States Forces Japan were he served as Secretary to the Joint Staff. During his service he graduated from the United States Command and General Staff School at Fort Leavenworth, Kansas; the Armed Forces Staff College at Norfolk, Virginia; and qualified as a paratrooper and Army Ranger. He retired from the Regular Army as a lieutenant colonel. He last assignment was as a Regular Army advisor with the 45th Infantry Brigade of the Oklahoma National Guard.He is the son of the author.

Reid Isaac Garrison is the son of Lieutenant Colonel Charles Alfred Garrison. He is a private in the 180th Infantry Regiment, 45th Infantry Brigade. He graduated from basic training at Fort Benning, Georgia, on March 8, 2002. His ambition is to carry on the Garrison tradition as a faithful Thunderbird. He is the grandson of the author and the son of Lieutenant Colonel Charles Garrison.

Cole Gordon Garrison, the youngest Thunderbird of them all and the son of Lieutenant Colonel Charles Alfred Garrison. He is a private in the 180th Infantry Regiment, 45th Infrantry Brigade. He is taking basic training at this time. He is the grandson of the author.

CHAPTER 39

WHAT WAS ACCOMPLISHED?

In retrospect, after all these years, it occurs to me that through our service in Korea we really did something of importance back there when the world was teetering near the abyss of a third world war. Looking back, it is easy to see that Joseph Stalin was one of the real villains of history. He was ready to plunge the world into darkness in order to achieve a complete communist take-over. The Korean War was our last chance to stop the advance of that godless creed. If the communists had won in Korea, we would live in a far different world today. Stalin was stopped. The later Soviet leaders were pale in comparison to the archenemy Stalin.

Those five Soviet Airborne Divisions stationed in Siberia only a few miles from the Japanese home islands were there for a purpose. I will always believe that the presence of the Thunderbird Division in early 1951 may well have stymied the Soviet plans for occupying Hokkaido, the northern most island of Japan. If Hokkaido had fallen, all of Japan would probably have gone behind the Iron Curtain. Perhaps the 45th presence on Hokkaido helped forestall a Soviet airborne assault. We may have been the "Cavalry arriving just in time," to put it in the vernacular of the Western frontier we all know about. At any rate, I truly believe that our occupation of Hokkaido might have been just as important to history as the service we later rendered in Korean combat. I remember the remark of Lieutenant Colonel Otwa T. Autry, the beloved and hard-bitten commander of the 189th Field

Artillery Battalion. He wryly looked at me and said, "You know old Joe Stalin must be quaking in his boots when we flaunt our four National Guard divisions in his face!" In retrospect, he may not have been quaking, but Stalin never unleashed his airborne units against Hokkaido. Maybe we accomplished that by our presence. I like to think so.

Then there were the Chinese. They gave us a real bloody nose up at the Chosin Reservoir when they suddenly came into the war. Their numbers alone were staggering. Those Marines and Army troops who fought a costly fighting retreat to Hungnam bought us time to finally stabilize the line and drive the communists, North Korean and Chinese alike, out of almost all of South Korea. We found that we could, indeed, give a good account of ourselves against the Chinese hordes. We whipped them, and finally saved South Korea. Our firepower taught the Chinese a lesson they still ponder. Their losses were

A 105-mm. howitzer on display at the 45th Infantry Division Museum in Oklahoma City, Oklahoma. Note that the howitzer was once used by Battery A, 171st Field Artillery Battalion. This weapon was the artillery backbone of the American infantry division in World War II and Korea.

A towed eight-inch howitzer on display at the 45th Infantry Division Museum in Oklahoma City, Oklahoma. This huge and accurate weapon generally was recognized to be the best artillery piece of World War II and Korea. It also proved itself in the Vietnam War. Usually it was in support of several divisions across and entire corps front. This weapon also was manufactured as a self-propelled howitzer.

Note the complicated mechanisms needed to properly aim and fire this weapon shown in this rear view of a 105-mm. howitzer at the 45th Infantry Division Museum in Oklahoma City. A full crew for this howitzer was made up of seven cannoneers. Its maximum range was 12,000 yards, or almost 7 miles. Battery B, 171st Field Artillery, was equipped with this type of howitzer.

calamitous, and they have never forgotten that. To this very day, the sacrifices of the American fighting man on the Korean Peninsula are influencing the Chinese and the North Koreans. We proved that we could, indeed, effectively operate as an army in the forbidding cold and harsh climate and terrain of Korea, against the best they could throw against us.

It is probable that the so-called Cold War would never have been won in the end, without the efforts and sacrifices of the American fighting man in the cold and bleak Korean War.

We stood and took losses, and gave out more than we received. We held the line. We staved off a third world war. At least, that is the way we look at it!

CONCLUSION

The 45th Infantry Division was tested in two of our country's wars. We can be proud the record made by the Thunderbirds.

First combat for the Thunderbird Division was in Sicily during World War II. This campaign was followed by a costly route of valor across Europe, from one end to the other. In World War II the 45th Division was in the following campaigns.

SICILY
NAPLE-FOGIA
ANZIO
SOUTHERN FRANCE
RHINELAND
ARDENNES-ALSACE
CENTRAL EUROPE

During these campaigns 45th Division soldiers won eight Medals of Honor and many other decorations for valor.

The 45th Division was in combat in Europe for 511 days during World War II.

In Korea, the 45th Division was in the following campaigns:

SECOND KOREAN WINTER
KOREA, SUMMER-FALL 1952
THIRD KOREAN WINTER
KOREA, SUMMER-FALL 1953

During these campaigns, 45th Division soldiers won one Medal of Honor and an astounding total of 27 Distinguished Service Crosses, the second ranking Army medal for valor.

During these Korean campaigns, the 45th Division was in combat for 429 days.

Very few Regular Army divisions, and no National Guard divisions, have a comparable record. The valor of the Thunderbirds has been spread over two continents, and never has a Thunderbird strategically retreated in all those days of combat.

General George S. Patton knew the 45th Division well. After the successful fight for Sicily, "Old Blood and Guts" had this to say to the assembled Thunderbirds: "Born at sea, baptized in blood, your fame shall never die. Your division is one of the best, if not the best, division in the history of American arms." If anyone knew about such things it was Georgie Patton as General Dwight D. Eisenhower called him. I'm proud to be a Thunderbird.

INDEX

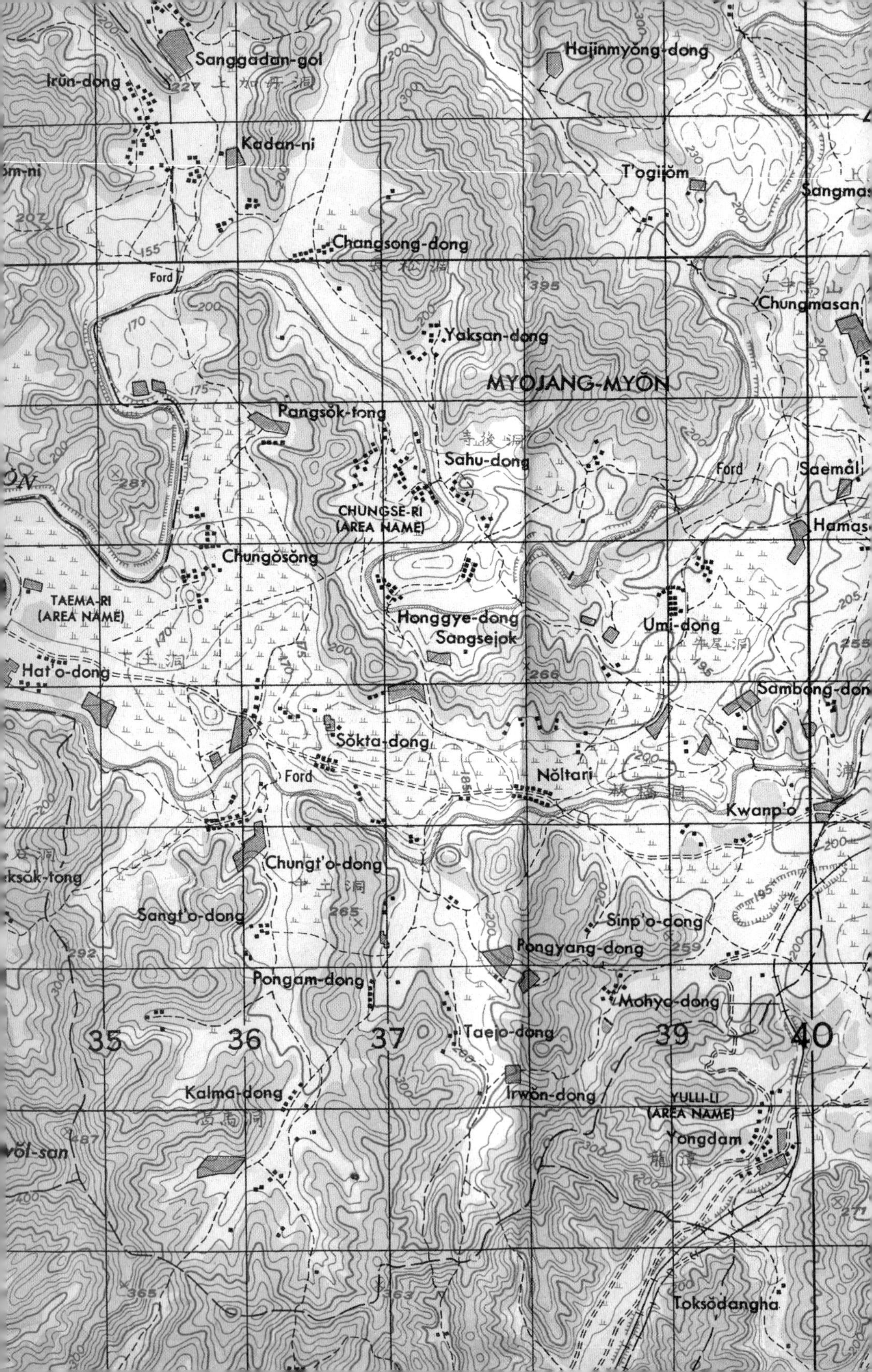

Sanggadan-gol
Irŭn-dong
Kadan-ni
Hajinmyŏng-dong
T'ogijŏm
Sangmas
Changsong-dong
Ford
Chungmasan
Yaksan-dong
MYOJANG-MYŎN
Pangsŏk-tong
Sahu-dong
CHUNGSE-RI
(AREA NAME)
Ford
Saemal
Hamas
Chungŏsŏng
TAEMA-RI
(AREA NAME)
Honggye-dong
Sangsejok
Umi-dong
Hat'o-dong
Sambong-don
Sŏkta-dong
Ford
Nŏltari
Kwanp'o
Chungt'o-dong
Sangt'o-dong
Sinp'o-dong
Pongyang-dong
Pongam-dong
Mohyo-dong
Taejo-dong
35
36
37
39
40
Kalma-dong
Irwŏn-dong
YULLI-LI
(AREA NAME)
Yongdam
Toksŏdangha